"And Then Fuzzy Told Seve..."

"And Then Fuzzy Told Seve..."

A Collection of the Best True Golf Stories Ever Told

DON WADE
Foreword by Curtis Strange

CB
CONTEMPORARY BOOKS
A TRIBUNE COMPANY

Library of Congress Cataloging-in-Publication Data

Wade, Don.
  "And then Fuzzy told Seve . . ." : a collection of the
best true golf stories ever told / Don Wade ; foreword by
Curtis Strange.
      p.   cm.
  Includes index.
  ISBN 0-8092-3273-1
    1. Golf—Anecdotes.   2. Golf players—Anecdotes.
  I. Title.
  GV967.W256   1996
  796.352—dc20   96-7800
                                                           CIP

Illustrations by Paul Szep

Copyright © 1996 by Don Wade
All rights reserved
Published by Contemporary Books
An imprint of NTC/Contemporary Publishing Company
Two Prudential Plaza, Chicago, Illinois 60601-6790
Manufactured in the United States of America
International Standard Book Number: 0-8092-3273-1
10   9   8   7   6   5   4   3   2

This one's for all the friends
I've met through golf.

CONTENTS

FOREWORD

I consider myself a very lucky guy, especially when it comes to golf. Because my father, Tom, was a professional, I learned the fundamentals early on. He also taught me the importance of sportsmanship and a respect for tradition that sets golf apart from so many other sports. And because my twin brother, Allan, was a really good player, I learned the value of competition pretty quickly. Sometimes our competitiveness would carry over from the golf course to the kitchen table, which didn't make my mother any too happy.

Since Dad was a pro, he always had plenty of stories to tell about the game and the people who played it. It didn't hurt that he was friends with players like Sam Snead, Chandler Harper, and Arnold Palmer. Listening to Dad's stories—some funny, some sad, some just plain amazing— helped give me a special feeling for the game. And it didn't hurt that when I went off to college at Wake Forest, my coach was Jesse Haddock, another great storyteller.

Somebody once said that in sports, the smaller the ball, the better the writing. If that's true, it may be because the smaller the ball, the more the player is out there on his own. Or her own. And since golf is an individual sport, the highs are higher and the lows lower. Your emotions are laid out there for everyone to see. There's not really any place to hide. There's nobody to blame but yourself.

It's that pure emotion that Don Wade has captured in this book and in the series of books that came before it. Beginning with *"And Then Jack Said to Arnie . . ."* and followed by *"And Then Arnie Told Chi Chi . . ."* and *"And Then Chi Chi Told Fuzzy . . ."*, these books will make you laugh. They will give you an insight into the great players. I hope they give you pause for reflection. More than anything else, I think they'll give you some great stories to share with your friends. Or with your kids. Just like my dad shared with me.

—Curtis Strange

PREFACE

As I write this, it's February and it's been a few months since I took a step away from life as a journalist. After seventeen years at *Golf Digest*, it was time to move on and, in a very real sense, move home. Coming back to Boston, where I was born and raised, is special. It's good to start closing the circle. And since Arnold, Fortuna, Lawner, and Cabot has me working on the advertising for Titleist and Foot-Joy, I'm still involved in the game.

It's no surprise, though, that as I stepped away from covering the game, I began to realize how much I miss it. The PGA Tour is at Pebble Beach this week, and I miss hanging around at one of the most beautiful places in America. I miss touching base with players I've known as friends for all these years. I miss catching up on the gossip with the crew from CBS and from the writers who cover the game. I miss the golf guys.

This is the fourth book in this series, and occasionally people ask if I ever tire of writing them. I don't, because working on these books constantly reminds me how special this game really is. The people. The places. The history. The link from one generation to the next. They're all part of the mix that make this more than a sport. To the extent that these books are able to capture a sense of that, then I think they've been successful.

And to the extent that these books have been successful, I owe a lot of thanks to a lot of people. First, my thanks to *Boston Globe* editorial cartoonist Paul Szep for his enduring friendship and his wonderful illustrations. Moving back to Boston was made a lot easier by having friends like Szeppy around. Steve Szurlej, from *Golf Digest*, again came through with a cover photograph that captures the camaraderie that is so much a part of the game. My long-suffering agent, Chris Tomasino, struggled to keep me on an even keel. That's what good agents do for their writers, and that's what Chris does better than most. Jerry Tarde, the editor of *Golf Digest*, was again supportive of my outside writing; but, more important, when the time came for me to move on, he asked me to stay on the masthead as a contributing editor. Thanks for that, and thanks to everyone at the magazine for their friendship. And thanks to Curtis Strange for writing the Foreword for this book. If I was Ryder Cup captain, I would want Curtis on my team. If I owned a publishing company, I would want Nancy Crossman to run the editorial side. She took a chance on *"And Then Jack Said to Arnie . . ."* and has been a great editor and an even better friend. Finally, there's the Gang of Wade—Julia, Ben, Darcy, and Andy. Thanks for all the love, patience, laughter, and understanding.

"And Then Fuzzy Told Seve..."

AMY ALCOTT

In a sense, it's a shame that Amy Alcott decided to play golf for a living, because that decision may have cost America a great comic actress. Maybe it's because she grew up in Los Angeles (or "The Land of the Birkenstock," as she calls it), but she has a natural comic timing, loves to be the center of attention, and is a world-class mimic.

Following the first round of the 1994 U.S. Women's Open at Indianwood Golf and Country Club outside Detroit, she was talking with a friend when a reporter from *Golf World* magazine, Pete McDaniel, asked if he could have a few minutes with her for a quick interview. She agreed, but asked her friend if he would rub her shoulders, which were beginning to tighten up.

As she and Pete talked, Amy's friend worked on her shoulders. After a few minutes, her muscles began to loosen.

"Oh, that feels so good," Amy said. "Keep it up."

The words were barely out of her mouth when she realized the comic possibilities. With a group of caddies, players and spectators looking on, she went into a nearly perfect re-creation of Meg Ryan's classic fake orgasm scene from the movie *When Harry Met Sally*. Naturally, it broke up the interview, and when she wandered away to the practice tee, she got a standing ovation from the crowd.

THE ARCHITECTS

One of America's most accomplished and eccentric golf course architects, A. W. Tillinghast, was born into a wealthy family from Philadelphia, and essentially led a life of aristocratic leisure. He married well, dabbled in the arts and literature and such sports as were suited to a gentleman of his social circles. Happily, one of those pastimes was golf, at which he was quite good. As a young man, he routinely traveled to St. Andrews in the summers to take lessons from Old Tom Morris, the club's professional, and played in several U.S. Amateurs.

His introduction to golf course architecture—and, not coincidentally, a real job—came in his early thirties when a friend asked him to design a course on the family's farm.

It turned out that Tillinghast had a natural affinity for the job, and given his society connections along the East Coast, he soon became a huge success, earning millions of dollars in fees. And with good reason, for Tillinghast was responsible for some of the country's finest courses— Winged Foot East and West, Quaker Ridge, the Upper and Lower courses at Baltusrol, Somerset Hills, Bethpage Black, and Ridgewood, to name just a few.

Alas, the Great Depression and some dubious investments combined to decimate Tillinghast's fortune. He eventually moved to Los Angeles and opened an antique shop whose inventory was based largely on pieces from his family's elaborate collections. This venture failed, and he eventually died in relative obscurity at the age of sixty-seven.

Tillinghast had little patience for critics of his courses—or of himself, for that matter. When the U.S. Open came to Winged Foot's West Course, Tillinghast was at the championship to accept the praise he was justifiably due for creating such a great test of golf.

As he sat in the clubhouse talking with friends, a man came up to him and said, "There's something wrong with your bunkers. A player just took four shots to get his ball out of one."

"Did it ever occur to you that the problem might not be with the bunkers?" Tillinghast sniffed.

Legend has it that architect Charles Blair MacDonald never accepted a fee for designing a golf course. He simply settled for a membership. Of course, given some of the courses he designed—the National Golf Links, Mid-Ocean Club, and the Yale University Golf Club—that wasn't all that bad an arrangement.

A rchitect Robert Trent Jones, Jr., learned many lessons from his father, who is perhaps the most well-known of all the golf course architects of the modern era. Not the least of those lessons was that golf is a universal game and that sometimes means building courses in out-of-the-way places—as long as the money is right.

One such place was Malaysia, where the younger Jones was commissioned to carve a course out of the steaming jungle. As he was doing his preliminary site research, he and a local guide had to wade through a swamp. Midway through, he saw a snake slither past as his guide quickly pulled out his machete.

"What kind of snake is that?" Jones asked.

"It's a krait snake," the guide answered.

"What happens if he bites you?" Jones said.

"You smoke one cigarette and say good-bye," the guide replied.

L ater in the same project, Jones and a member of his crew were driving to the course site when they encountered an elephant resting in the middle of the road. The crew member, who was driving, stopped the car, got out, and quietly approached the elephant. When he was next to the animal he spoke very softly to it, and moments later the elephant rose to its feet and wandered off.

When the man returned to the car, Jones asked him what he had said.

"Lord of the jungle, may we pass?" the man answered.

"How do you know that the elephant understood what you were saying?" Jones asked.

"He understands me because I respect him," the man said.

On another occasion Jones was hired to design a course in Bangkok. The head of the Thai Military Bank, which was financing the development, took him on a boat cruise. Jones took this to be a courtesy cruise, a chance for the two men to get to know each other. He was in for a surprise.

"Tell me, Mr. Navapan, where is the property we'll be building the course on?" Jones asked.

"You're floating on it," came the answer.

Not the least of the challenges Jones faced overseas came in Third World and economically depressed countries. In fact, one of his toughest assignments came when he was commissioned to build a golf course outside Moscow. In the end, the project took some twenty years to complete.

"When we were first starting the project I was walking through the woods with a compass and a topographical map the government had given us," Jones recalls. "It didn't take me very long to figure out that there was something wrong with the map. Finally, I asked one of the officials if the map was inaccurate."

"Yes, the map is incorrect," the man finally conceded. "We never give correct maps to foreigners because your military will use them to attack us."

"Well," Jones replied, "if you give me an incorrect map I will give you an incorrect golf course."

Eventually the officials produced a map so complete that it listed the circumference of every tree on the property. For his part, Jones paid a form of homage to the Russians' military history when he sculptured bunkers on the third hole of the Moscow Country Club out of old craters caused by German bombing during World War II.

A similar story comes from England. During World War II, Luftwaffe pilots dropped heavy bombs on Sunningdale, the lovely parkland course near London. After the war, the membership debated what to do with the craters near the right side of the 18th green.

With classic British common sense they elected to do the obvious: they made them into a fearsome bunker.

Robert Trent Jones, Sr., was hired to build a course near the Pyramids in Egypt. Early on in the project he was asked if he had any suggestions for naming the course.

"We could call it 'The Sphinx Links,'" he quipped.

Today, golf course architects routinely use computers and all sorts of state-of-the-art technology to design and build courses. That was far from the case with early architects. For example, Charles Blair MacDonald, who designed several of the world's greatest courses, including the National Golf Links on Long Island, had a unique method of determining the contours of his greens.

"I would take a number of smooth, round pebbles in my hand and drop them on a small space representing the putting green," he once explained. "I watched as they dropped on the diagram, and then placed the undulations accordingly."

Whereas today's architects often learn their skills in college, MacDonald—who was a man of some wealth—went back to his roots. Literally. For five summers he traveled to Great Britain and studied all the great courses, taking careful notes. It's not surprising, therefore, that several of the holes at the National resemble holes in the British Isles—particularly those at St. Andrews, where MacDonald attended university as a youth.

TOMMY ARMOUR

Players who complain about the severity of the greens at Augusta National should keep in mind the story of Tommy Armour playing in the 1937 Masters.

Armour, who won both the U.S. and British Opens as well as a PGA Championship, was obviously a complete player. Still, all his skill and experience wasn't enough as he stood over a difficult, twisting, downhill three-foot putt for par on the 10th green. He played this putt well enough, leaving the ball within inches of the hole.

Sadly, he wound up making one of the most embarrassing sixes in Masters history as he missed the next putt.

A similar misfortune befell Hale Irwin at the 1983 British Open at Royal Birkdale. He was playing the 198-yard, par-3 14th hole in the third round, and hit a good first putt, leaving his ball just an inch from the hole. Frustrated, he carelessly went to swipe it into the hole, but the head of his putter jammed into the turf short of the ball, and the putterhead hopped over the ball. Although the ball never moved, Irwin told his playing companion, Peter Oosterhuis, to mark him down for a bogey 4. It turned out to be a very costly mistake. The next day he finished one shot behind Tom Watson, tied for second with Andy Bean.

"Fortunately it wasn't an important tournament," Irwin joked later. "Just the British Open."

Armour knew the pressures of competition fully as well as anyone who has ever played the game. And he also understood that, unless you have been under that pressure, it is impossible to appreciate what it is like.

Armour was playing in a tournament in California in the early 1930s. He was paired with Johnny Revolta, who was fighting for a share of the lead. When Revolta left a four-footer a bit short of the hole, a man in the gallery yelled, "Gutless!"

Armour wheeled around and confronted the man.

"I'll bet you any amount of money you want that you couldn't make that putt," the icy Scotsman said.

"Don't be ridiculous," the man replied.

They settled on a $5,000 bet—an enormous amount of money in those days. The man went to the bank and withdrew his $5,000. Armour collected the same amount from his fellow professionals, who joined him and a growing gallery on the 18th green. Both men placed their cash on the green near the hole, and a ball was placed on the same spot from which Revolta had putted.

As the gallery closed in around him, the man addressed the ball and then backed off, sweating heavily and his hands visibly shaking. When he finally hit the putt, the ball wound up both wide and short of the hole.

"I want to apologize to Mr. Revolta," the man said. "When I got over the ball I couldn't even see the hole. I had no idea."

"In that case," said Armour, "the bet is off. Pick up your money."

AUGUSTA NATIONAL GOLF CLUB

Many people who attend the Masters leave with a souvenir, usually a shirt, hat, sweater, or something else from one of the numerous outdoor pro shops. But Bob Warters, who used to edit the British golf magazine *Today's Golfer*, had a better idea. He brought back a little bit of the course.

Walking the course on the last day of the tournament, he noticed a divot that had just been ripped from the fairway. Warters put it in his pocket, took it back with him to England, and carefully nurtured it with water, sunlight, and lawn food. Alas, it was to no avail. His little slice of Augusta never adjusted to English life.

Augusta might be the best-known course in the world, largely because of the annual telecasts of the Masters. But while people are familar with the holes on the back nine, they know less about the front nine, which doesn't receive nearly the same amount of coverage.

And although people know how difficult the par-3 12th and 16th are, they don't appreciate the danger that lurks on the 4th hole, a par 3 of just over 200 yards. But the players know, and Dr. Cary Middlecoff knows better than most.

Doc Middlecoff, who won the 1955 Masters and two U.S. Opens, came to the 4th hole one year and stood on the tee trying to make his club selection as the wind howled in his face. The wind was so strong that Doc pulled a driver from his bag, addressed the ball, and hit it right on the screws. This would have been fine except that just at the moment the ball streaked off the clubface, the wind died. The ball was still rising as it soared over the green. It carried into a tall stand of trees behind the green, flew over a fence, and finally landed out of bounds. Way out of bounds.

In 1991, Bruce Fleisher went to the Masters as a spectator. It must have been a bittersweet visit. In 1969, as the reigning U.S. Amateur champion, he was the low amateur at the tournament. Much was expected of Fleisher when he turned pro in 1970, but he had never won a tournament on the PGA Tour and had largely left the Tour by 1984 to work as a teaching professional. Fleisher was so far removed from the Tour that the 1991 media guide didn't list him, even as a marginal player.

With all that in mind, the people who were seated near him in the grandstands behind the practice tee at Augusta National must have been surprised—not to say astonished—when Fleisher announced that next year he'd be back inside the ropes as a player. But just a few months later Fleisher, forty-two, won the New England Classic in a seven-hole playoff with Australia's Ian Baker-Finch. Baker-Finch, it should be noted, was no journeyman; he went on to win the British Open two weeks later.

It would have been a storybook ending if Fleisher had won, or even challenged for, the green jacket. But he shot a very respectable 284 to wind up nine shots behind the winner, Fred Couples.

Still, in a very real sense, it was a victory.

SEVE BALLESTEROS

Surely, one of the most unlikely alliances in the history of golf was the teacher-pupil relationship between Mac O'Grady and Seve Ballesteros.

Ballesteros is quite simply a golf genius. He burst upon the golf scene when he finished second in the 1976 British Open at Birkdale at the tender age of nineteen. For the next fifteen years or so he shined as one of the game's brightest stars, winning three British Opens and two Masters. He played with an audacity and emotion that made him one of those few players who genuinely deserve the adjective "charismatic."

But by the early 1990s his wins were coming farther apart, and this most natural of talents began a frustrating search for the game that had so mysteriously left him. That search brought him to none other than Mac O'Grady—as enigmatic a player as has ever lived.

O'Grady, a child of southern California, endured seventeen trips through the Tour's qualifying school before he finally made it on tour. Once he made it, he won twice but never really seemed happy out there. He fought bitterly and publicly with then-Commissioner Deane Beman (at least one thing he and Seve had in common), endured his share of controversies and fines, and eventually lost interest in playing. He did not, however, lose interest in the mysteries of the swing and the game. He became something of a cult figure among players, and eventually he and Seve—who had been friends on tour anyway—began to work together.

"Seve and I get along very well," Mac once said. "He's the only person I know who is more neurotic than I am." No small statement from the man who once said that he liked watching America's daytime parade of human horror stories, the shows like *Geraldo* and *Oprah*, because they "prove there are people out there more screwed up than me."

At any rate, the two men got together in 1994 after Mac wrote Seve's mother offering his help. They began by visiting a beach so Seve could hit balls with the pure joy and abandon that he had as a boy in Spain. No swing theories. No complications. Just Seve, a club, and a ball—like the old days.

A year later, in Palm Desert, the two staged a mock funeral. They dug a grave and buried a box filled with photographs of Seve's old swing.

"It was a very happy funeral," Seve said. "I buried all my old habits. Now all I have left are my new ones."

Seve Ballesteros is a ferocious competitor. His play in the Ryder Cup proved to be an inspiration for the entire European team. It is a cliché to write that he is the heart and soul of the team, but it is not an exaggeration. Of course, in an atmosphere as charged as the Ryder Cup, sparks are bound to fly, and that's exactly what happened in a 1991 match between Seve and his partner, José-María

Olazábal, and Americans Paul Azinger and Chip Beck at the Ocean Course at Kiawah Island.

Early in the match the Europeans noticed that the Americans were alternating between 90- and 100-compression balls—a violation of the often-arcane Rules of Golf. When Ballesteros and Olazábal pointed out the infraction, Azinger—who is every bit as competitive as Ballesteros—protested.

"I can promise you we are not trying to cheat," Azinger said.

"Oh, no," Seve replied. "Cheating and breaking the rules are two different things."

DEANE BEMAN

Deane Beman is best known as the commissioner of the PGA Tour from 1974 until 1994, but before becoming commissioner he compiled an enviable record as a player. In six years on tour, he won four tournaments. As an amateur he won two U.S. Amateurs and a British Amateur and represented the United States on numerous international teams. Clearly, this is a man who knows something about competitive golf.

That's why he was astonished when he heard that in the 1990 U.S. Amateur at Cherry Hills, Phil Mickelson—who went on to win—gave his first-round opponent a ten-foot putt on the opening hole of their match.

"Either that kid can't add or he doesn't know anything about golf," Beman said.

TOMMY BOLT

Tommy Bolt was playing at Pebble Beach one year in the old Bing Crosby National Pro-Am. He stood on the tee preparing to hit his shot when some deer wandered onto the fairway. Bolt backed off and waited until the deer left. Then he set back up over the ball, only to look and see the deer return. When it happened a third time, it was too much for Bolt to take.

"Where the hell are the marshals?" he asked.

Like many players, Tommy has an acute sense of hearing—especially if he's not playing very well.

One afternoon he was struggling through a round, and as he prepared to putt he was distracted by a woman rummaging through her purse. The rattling of keys and tinkling of small change finally became more than he could stand.

"Lady, would you give me a break?" he asked. "How would you like it if I came into your kitchen and started cracking my knuckles while you were making dinner?"

JOHN BREDEMUS

Travel outside of Texas and the name John Bredemus might not mean much, but in the state that has produced the likes of Ben Hogan, Byron Nelson, Jimmy Demaret, Dave Marr, Tom Kite, and Ben Crenshaw, he is nothing less than legend.

Bredemus was born and raised in a life of wealth and comfort. He went to Dartmouth and Princeton, and was a member of the 1912 U.S. Olympic team, finishing second to Jim Thorpe in the decathlon competition. It is said that Thorpe entrusted Bredemus with his athletic medals in the years just prior to his death, and that Bredemus eventually had them melted down to help pay off some of his debts.

Bredemus, who should have fit so easily among the society swells of the Northeast, chose instead to move to Texas. He became a high school teacher in San Antonio and eventually became an assistant professional at the city's Brackenridge Park Golf Course.

Bredemus went on to help found both the PGA of America and the Texas chapter of the PGA, and he was the key to getting the Texas Open up and running. He eventually went on to design hundreds of courses in Texas, the best being the Colonial Country Club in Fort Worth—the site of the Colonial National Invitation and the 1941 U.S. Open.

For all his success as a golf course architect, he was nearly penniless at the time of his death from a heart attack in 1946. His family, which had effectively disowned him, refused to pay for his funeral, so the members of the Texas PGA took up a collection to pay for the services.

FRANCIS H. I. BROWN

Francis Brown was born in Hawaii, the heir to one of the largest fortunes on the island. He was an outstanding athlete, and golf was the sport that he loved more than any other. Fortunately, he had plenty of time to practice, since he was never exactly burdened with a day job.

In 1930, he qualified for the U.S. Amateur at Merion. He brought along many of his wealthiest friends, and they all rented houses bordering holes on Merion's back nine.

It is a testimony to Brown's skill that several of them laid down enormous bets that Brown would win the medal for the lowest qualifying score. This in the tournament that Bobby Jones would win to complete his historic sweep of the U.S. and British Opens and Amateurs—the "Grand Slam."

Brown started out very well, and after the first round he was among the leaders for medalist honors. He continued playing very well the next day—until he reached the back nine, when his instinctive conviviality took over. The 14th and 15th holes sat across the street from the houses Brown's friends had rented for the week. Somehow—and it doesn't seem as it took too much effort—Brown was persuaded to stop in for a drink. One drink led to another, and Brown never made it back to the course to complete his round.

Like many people who are born into a lot of money, Brown was somewhat absentminded about how much cash he carried around. Most times, of course, this wasn't a problem, but occasionally it got him into a jam.

One evening he was out on the town in Honolulu, and after buying round after round of drinks for his friends, the bar bill came and he found he was tapped out. "No problem," he assured the bartender. "I sold some land this morning and I've got the check right here. Can you cash it?"

With that he pulled a check from his wallet. It was from the Treasurer of the United States of America in the amount of $6,000,000.00.

Brown loved Scotland and traveled there often. On one trip he was playing at Gleneagles and made a hole-in-one. He sent word back to the clubhouse that the drinks were on him until five that afternoon. Naturally, word spread across the surrounding countryside, and the locals were more than happy to join in the celebration. To make matters worse—or better, depending on your point of view—in all the excitement and celebration, he forgot to tell the barman to close down the bar.

The next day he received a bill for more than $5,000, which he happily paid. To this day, he is held in almost universal regard as one of the greatest Yanks who ever visited this part of Scotland.

Whatever dreams Brown harbored of being a top amateur player ended with a horrible car crash in 1935. Brown was a passenger in a car that smashed into a tree at high speed. The car was totaled. One passenger was declared dead at the scene by police. Brown was rushed to the hospital, and was eventually taken to the morgue. As a sheet was being pulled over his face, he somehow contrived to wiggle his foot. He was rushed back to the emergency room, where doctors managed to save his life.

CADDIES

An American arrived at St. Andrews for his first round at the Old Course. What with St. Andrews being the Home of Golf, he approached this as being an almost religious experience and, having heard so much about the caddies at St. Andrews, he took great pains to make sure he could get one of the veteran caddies to carry his bag.

When the time came to approach the first tee, he met his caddie for the first time. It wasn't a pretty sight. Instead of the romanticized version of the caddies he'd imagined, he found a poster boy for Alcoholics Anonymous. Still, he held out hope until he hit his opening drive.

So nervous he could barely see, he lurched at the ball and made only the most fleeting of contact.

"Where'd it go?" he anxiously asked his caddie.

"Where'd what go, sir?" the caddie answered.

Caddying has long been a popular way to make a living for immigrants to this country, particularly in the large urban areas along the East Coast.

25

Winged Foot Golf Club outside New York City was one club that benefited from a ready pool of men new to this country. They might not have known much about the game, but they were willing to work hard and enjoyed being outside instead of in a factory.

One day a new caddie was walking up a fairway on the West course. As he approached the green, his golfer asked for his sand wedge. The caddie seemed to ignore him, walking stoically ahead with his head down. The man asked again for his sand wedge, and again got no reaction. After the third request the caddie stopped, laid the bag down, and reached inside one of the pockets, pulling out a brown bag.

"All right," he said in his heavily accented English as he reached inside the bag and pulled out a sandwich wrapped in paper. "But only half. I've got to eat too."

One of the surprise leaders in the early rounds of the 1995 British Open was Japan's Katsuyoshi Tomori. In an interview he credited his Scottish caddie for his fine play. This baffled the writers, since Tomori spoke no English and his caddie spoke no Japanese. How, the writers wondered, did they communicate?

"He points very well," Tomori explained through an interpreter.

WINSTON CHURCHILL

By any standard, Winston Churchill was a man of uncommon courage. He risked death as a young man in escaping from prison during the Boer War, and then personified British resolve in leading his nation against the Nazi assault in the early days of World War II. And while he was an avid sportsman, he never much fancied golf. Alistair Cooke, the graceful British writer and commentator, knew enough about both Churchill and golf to hazard a guess as to why Churchill avoided the game.

"He was not willing to suffer public displays of humiliation," Cooke said, in a brief but brilliant description of the game of golf.

Although Churchill was not an avid golfer by any stretch of the imagination, he enjoyed a membership at Walton Heath, the exclusive club in Walton-on-the-Hill outside London. In the years prior to World War I, Churchill was one of twenty-four Members of Parliament who had memberships at the club.

One day he chanced to play with David Lloyd George, then the Prime Minister. As was the custom there was a small wager on the outcome of the match, but as Churchill stood over his putt on the final green, he upped the ante.

"I shall now putt you for the Prime Minister's office," Churchill said.

He missed, but the rest, as they say, is history.

FRED COUPLES

Fred Couples is one of the game's most popular players, and with good reason. He's easygoing and genuinely friendly, and if he has a reputation for not taking life too seriously, that's fine with him. Jim Nantz, who went to the University of Houston with Fred and is one of his best friends, tells a story about a phone call he once had with Fred.

Couples had taken six weeks off in 1995 to rest his back. In the course of their conversation, Nantz asked Couples if the time off had been boring.

"No, not really," said Couples. "I've almost finished my book."

"I didn't know you were writing a book," Nantz said.

"I'm not," Couples said. "I'm reading one."

One of the most poignant moments in Masters history came in 1992, when Fred Couples won the tournament—his first Major championship.

After he signed his scorecard, tournament officials

brought him to the CBS studio in Butler Cabin, where he would be interviewed by Jim Nantz and awarded the Green Jacket by the 1991 winner, Ian Woosnam.

What made the moment so special was that Nantz and Couples had been through this many times before in mock interviews. As suitemates at Houston, Nantz—who dreamed of covering the Masters for CBS—would "interview" Couples—who dreamed of winning the Masters one day.

After CBS went off the air, Couples and Nantz embraced, both with tears in their eyes.

"The thing that is so amazing is that all those years ago, we always knew it was going to be the Masters that Fred would win," Nantz said.

BEN CRENSHAW

Ben Crenshaw's emotional victory in the 1995 Masters was one of the most popular wins in the Majors in recent memory. And nobody was happier for him than Linn Strickler, his regular tour caddie, who watched the tournament at home.

For most of the Masters's history, players were required to use caddies from Augusta National. That changed in 1983, when players were permitted to use their regular caddies. One player who resisted the change was Crenshaw, who still has Carl Jackson, an Augusta National caddie, carrying his bag. That being the case, Strickler found himself at home with a week off, which, naturally he spent watching the Masters on television.

In the final round, Crenshaw dueled with Davis Love III, who was playing ahead of him. The result was very much up in the air until Crenshaw made a twelve-foot birdie putt on the 17th hole.

When the ball fell into the hole, Strickler leaped out of his chair and jumped into the air with joy—and also with considerable pain, as his left hand smashed into the ceiling fan churning above him.

Strickler spent the rest of the tournament cheering for Ben from the bathroom, where he tried to bandage his bleeding hand over the sink.

After putting out on 18, an emotionally spent Crenshaw embraced his wife, Julie. Both of them had tears streaming down their faces.

"This Green Jacket is for Claire," the two-time Masters champion told his wife, referring to their second child.

They returned home late that night, and after a couple of hours sleep, Crenshaw took his oldest daughter, Katherine, to school. He brought a little something with him for show-and-tell—his second Green Jacket.

Ben Crenshaw is one of those rare players, like Sam Snead and Seve Ballesteros, who have a genius for the game. More than almost any other top golfer, he plays by feel and instinct. And although his play has been praised ever since he was a teenager growing up in Austin, Texas, he is self-deprecating about his abilities.

One day in the mid-1970s a writer asked him how far he felt he was from being a great player.

"About five inches," he quipped. "The distance between my right ear and my left ear."

NATHANIEL CROSBY

Match play competitions are almost always more unpre-
dictable than medal events, but the 1981 U.S. Amateur
at San Francisco's Olympic Club will go down as one of the
most unusual in the history of the championship. Many of
the top players were eliminated in the early rounds, and it
soon became obvious that the biggest story of the week
would be the play of Nathaniel Crosby, the son of the late
Bing Crosby.

Nathaniel, who was attending the University of Miami,
had grown up in nearby Burlingame, California, and had
learned the game by playing with his father at Burlingame
Country Club. He was a talented player, but few gave him
much of a chance against the likes of Hal Sutton, Jay Sigel,
and Willie Wood. It was an unusually strong field, because
the Walker Cup had been played the week before at Cypress
Point.

Nathaniel displayed a fine short game and a gritty tenac-
ity, but many thought his ball-striking was suspect and
would betray him in the later brackets. But he converted a
lot of skeptics as he played his way into the finals against
Brian Lindley.

In that final, however, it looked as though Nathaniel's
luck had run out. He was one down after the morning 18

and then slipped to four down after the first seven holes in the afternoon. But he rallied to level the match, forcing a playoff that he won with a birdie on the first extra hole.

In the postmatch interview he gave writers an insight into what drove him to succeed.

"My father was a success," he said. "My mother [an actress] was a success. My brother made it. Heck, my sister [Mary, an actress in the television series *Dallas*] even shot J.R. That's a tough act to follow."

From his boyhood, Nathaniel Crosby mixed easily with famous golfers. Toney Penna, the celebrated player and clubmaker, became his coach. Ben Crenshaw was a frequent partner in the tournament started by his father. And then there was Ben Hogan.

Hogan frequently traveled to Florida and stayed with his friend, George Coleman—an old friend of the Crosby family. On one visit, Nathaniel happened to be spending the night. The next morning the teenager was walking down the hallway carrying a hair dryer.

"What the hell is that thing?" a bewildered Hogan asked.

CYPRESS POINT CLUB

In survey after survey, when people are asked to name the course they would play if they had just one course to play for the rest of their lives, invariably the one most often selected is Cypress Point, on the Monterey Peninsula. There are certainly more difficult courses, but there isn't a course in the world that can match Cypress Point for sheer physical beauty. The course winds through forest and vast sand dunes, but it is the holes along the ocean that define Cypress Point, especially the back-to-back par 3s—15 and 16—which are two of the most dramatic and photogenic holes in all of golf.

The 15th hole is a short hole of some 140 yards to a well-bunkered green. It requires a shot over a dramatic inlet, but since it usually calls for a short iron, the water is rarely a factor, especially for good players.

The 16th, however, is a completely different story. It's more than 230 yards long, and almost all of that is over yet another inlet. To make matters worse, the prevailing wind is in the player's face, meaning that even the best players are often looking at a driver—to a relatively small green. The margin for error is reduced even more by the sheer rock cliffs that front the green and the unforgiving ice plants that grow along those cliffs.

"It's just one mean hole," Sam Snead explained one day, describing the 16th hole at Cypress Point. "It's like that beautiful woman you know is going to break your heart but you can't stay away because she's so pretty. Next thing you know, you're in over your head.

"I remember one year—1953, I think—Porky Oliver came to that hole playing pretty well. The wind was just howling dead into your face. He hit five balls in a row into the ocean, and then put the sixth ball into the ice plant. Hell, you just can't play from that stuff. Well, old Porky wound up making a 16. It took a lot to get Porky hot, but he was plenty mad when he came off the course that day."

In 1957, Gardner Dickinson came to the hole and left his tee shot down on the beach below the steep cliffs. By the time he was through, he had taken a 9 and shot himself out of the tournament. Still, according to Dickinson, there have been players who have suffered worse indignities.

"Henry Ransom hit it down on the beach one day and tried to play it back up to the green," Dickinson said. "The ball smashed off the cliffs and hit him in the chest. He told his caddie to pick up the ball and walked in.

"'When they start hitting back at you it's time to quit,' he said," Dickinson recalled.

That's not to say that the hole can't be had. No less a figure than Bing Crosby—a longtime member of the club—made a hole-in-one with a driver one afternoon in 1947.

"It might not have been the best shot I ever hit," said Crosby. "But I got more publicity from it than from any other shot I've ever played."

The 17th hole at Cypress Point is not as well-known as the 16th, but it's seen its share of history. It's a 375-yard par 4 with the ocean running down the entire right side and a clump of gnarled old Cypress trees in the fairway, blocking the approach to the green for drives played to the right center of the fairway. In 1951, Byron Nelson found himself blocked out by these trees.

To the astonishment of his caddie, fellow players, and the gallery, Nelson aimed his approach shot directly out over the Pacific and hit a hard hook. The ball tore off the club-face and rose out over the rocks and the water. As it ballooned into the wind, the ball seemed to hang in the air and then began to fall sharply to the left as it lost momentum. It came to rest on the green, and Nelson wound up making a par.

JIMMY DEMARET

A writer once asked Jimmy Demaret why he thought golf held such a fascination for so many people. If the writer was looking for a deeply cosmic explanation, he had come to the wrong guy.

"Golf and sex are the only two things you can enjoy without doing either of them very well," he explained.

One of Jimmy Demaret's best friends was Don Cherry. This was only natural, since Cherry was a Texan, a fine amateur golfer, and a popular singer. Demaret and Cherry had a lot in common. The difference was that Demaret got paid for his golf and Cherry got paid for his singing.

Cherry showed up at Demaret's club—the Champions Golf Club in Houston—during the 1967 Ryder Cup matches. He was shooting a movie at the time and had shaved his head and grown a beard for the part.

When Demaret saw Cherry, he couldn't help himself.

"Don," he said. "You look great, but your head is on upside down."

Demaret teamed with Jackie Burke, Jr., the former Masters and PGA champion, to build the Champions Golf Club. When the construction was finished a van arrived with furniture for the clubhouse. One of the workers asked Demaret where to put Burke's desk, and Demaret thought about it for a second.

"Put it on the practice tee," he said. "That's where Jackie spends all his time anyway."

And they did.

DAVID FEHERTY

Ireland's David Feherty brought a quick wit with him when he came to America to play on the PGA Tour. A writer once asked him if he played for the love of the game or just for the money.

"Neither, actually," he said. "I play the game because my sole ambition is to do well enough to give it up."

One year Feherty came to Massachusetts to play in the New England Classic, not far from Boston—arguably the most Irish city in America. He was asked if he enjoyed playing in the tournament.

"Very much so," he said. "It's like playing in the Irish Open, except there are more Irish people in the galleries here."

When word spread that his marriage was in trouble, a friend approached Feherty and asked him if he'd lost weight.

"Yes, 150 pounds . . . 135 of them being my wife," he said. "I call it my Divorce Diet."

RALPH GULDAHL

When the subject of great players comes up, one name that is rarely mentioned is Ralph Guldahl, but for a time he was as good as anyone who was playing the game. He won the U.S. Open in 1937 and 1938. He won the 1939 Masters after finishing second the two previous years. On top of that, he won three straight Western Opens, which were then considered on a par with the Masters in terms of importance. Then, mysteriously, his game seemed to vanish. Some people claimed it was because he had authored an instruction book, causing him to actually think about the mechanics of the game for the first time. Sam Snead disagrees.

"Goldie took some time off, and when he came back he had the most god-awful–looking grip you've ever seen," Snead explained. "It's hard to believe that a man could go from having a perfect grip to one that bad. I tried to help him fix it, but he just couldn't do it. He was lost."

In the 1937 U.S. Open at Oakland Hills, Sam Snead was in the clubhouse following his final round. The only person who could catch him was Ralph Guldahl, but it would be tough. He needed to par the last six holes to force a play-off, and the closing holes at Oakland Hills are one of the toughest stretches in the game. Guldahl was magnificent, birdieing two of the six holes.

As he waited to putt out on the last green, he calmly pulled a comb from his pocket and ran it through his hair.

"Why shouldn't I have combed my hair?" he asked later. "I had a two-shot lead and I knew my picture was going to be in all the papers the next day."

WALTER HAGEN

In 1933, after his glory days were over, Walter Hagen decided to play in the U.S. Open, more as a lark and a chance to see old friends than anything else.

On the eve of the Open, Gene Sarazen wrote a newspaper column suggesting that it was a mistake for his old friend and rival to risk damaging his reputation by playing in the Open. Sarazen suggested that Hagen should "sit back in an easy chair and enjoy the Open."

Surprisingly—or maybe not surprisingly, considering it was Walter Hagen—he played pretty well, and in the final round even turned in a 66.

As Hagen relaxed over a drink in the clubhouse following his round, word came from the course that Sarazen was struggling and had played his way out of contention. Hagen summoned a member of the clubhouse staff, gave him a handful of dollar bills, and sent him on his way.

A short while later, the man met Sarazen on the course, placed an armchair next to him on the tee, and said, "Your easy chair, sir, from Mr. Hagen."

A writer once asked Hagen how he made a birdie on a particularly tough par 5.

"Easy," said Hagen. "Three of them and one of these."

By the time the 1940 PGA Championship rolled around, Hagen was well past his prime. Still, the tournament offered a chance to see old friends, and he decided to play. This did not mean, however, that he had any intention of cutting back on his partying.

Before his first match, against Gil Sellers, he arrived at the course still reeling from the effects of the previous evening. Meeting Sellers, he told him to start without him.

"I'll give you the first two holes and catch up with you," Hagen said.

Despite starting out two down and with a hangover, Hagen went on to win, 1-up.

During the U.S. Open one year, Hagen was paired with a young player in the first round. The player, showing the effects of the pressure, three-putted the first green.

"Don't worry, kid," Hagen said. "If you three-putt the first green, they'll never remember. But if you three-putt the last green, they'll never forget."

Hagen came to the final hole of the 1923 British Open at Royal Troon needing a birdie to tie Arthur Havers. He hit a good drive but shanked his approach shot into a greenside bunker.

With an enormous gallery surrounding the green, Hagen entered the bunker, studied the contour of the green, and then plumb-bobbed the shot with his club. After all of that, he came within inches of holing the shot and forcing a playoff.

In the 1926 British Open at Royal Lytham and St. Annes, Hagen needed an eagle 2 on the last hole to tie Bobby Jones. A good drive left him 150 yards from the hole. Once he reached his ball, he and his caddie walked all the way to the green, where Hagen studied the area around the hole. He pulled an iron from the bag and told his caddie to tend the pin. Hagen then walked back to his ball and hit the shot, almost holing the ball on the fly.

Hagen was the captain of the 1933 Ryder Cup team, which would travel to Southport, England, for the matches. In those days, the team sailed from New York City amid great publicity.

When the team arrived in New York a few days prior to departure, Hagen took one look at their clothes and was appalled. He ordered the entire team to visit the finest tailors in the city for new wardrobes. And then he had the bills sent to the fledgling PGA of America.

To say that Hagen was a confident, even cocky, player is a huge understatement. As captain of the 1929 Ryder Cup team, he paired himself against the captain of the British/Irish team, George Duncan, then forty-five.

"Boys, there's a point for our side," he told his team.

Duncan went on to win, 10 and 8, the most lopsided victory in Ryder Cup history.

Many years after his retirement, Hagen decided to try to play again. His first attempts weren't very successful, in part because he had done absolutely nothing to stay in shape but largely because his eyesight had worsened with age. A friend suggested he try to find a pair of glasses that would correct his vision. A few days later Hagen returned to the golf course with six pairs of glasses.

"If none of these sons of bitches work, so be it," he said. None of them did, and Hagen never played again.

PHIL HARRIS

Phil Harris, the singer and entertainer who died in 1995, was a fixture at Pebble Beach over the years. In fact, he teamed with Dutch Harrison to win the Crosby in 1954.

In the final round, Harris hit his drive on the par-3 17th on the green but some ninety feet from the hole. Then he sank the putt for a two net one. Later, a writer asked him how long the putt was.

"I don't know, son, but I'd like to have that much land on Wilshire Boulevard," he quipped.

CLAYTON HEAFNER

Clayton Heafner was a wonderful player with possibly the shortest fuse the game has ever seen. Most of the time he directed his anger at himself or tournament officials, but on one occasion the stress of having a particularly inept pro-am partner got to be too much.

After struggling through a round that could only be described as torturous, he came to one of the closing holes. The clubhouse was in sight, and within it a much-needed drink to calm his nerves. His amateur partner, after hitting another poor drive, went to great pains to size up his approach shot.

"What do you think, pro?" he asked. "Should I lay up or go for it?"

"Neither," said Heafner. "Put it in your pocket and let's get out of here."

BEN HOGAN

Unlike some other great players who went on to establish reputations as skilled teachers—most notably Byron Nelson—Ben Hogan never cared much for working with other players. He would teach by example, and if anyone was willing to pay attention, then so much the better for them. His work ethic was there for all to see, and his advice was simple:

"The answer is in the dirt. Go dig it out," he always said.

Still, on occasion, he would be moved to offer advice.

Jan Stephenson used to practice at Shady Oaks, Hogan's home course in Fort Worth. When Hogan was practicing she would watch him from a discreet distance, never daring to ask questions or even make small talk with him. One day, after she had just lost a tournament by skying to a 77 in the final round, he invited her to come over to his spot on the practice tee.

"Hit some," he said.

Stephenson—by her own admission "choking like a rat"—began working her way through her bag.

"I had studied his practice routine and I did everything exactly the same way he did," she recalled. "I kept waiting for him to say something. Finally, I couldn't take it anymore, and I asked him what he thought."

"How the hell can you ever shoot a 77 with that swing?" he said as he got in his cart and drove away.

Another player Hogan took an interest in is Kris Tschetter, a talented young LPGA player who went to Texas Christian University in Fort Worth.

After a particularly good tournament she was approached by writers who wanted to learn more about her friendship with Ben Hogan.

"Could you tell us what you work on with Mr. Hogan?" a writer asked.

"I could tell you, of course," she laughed. "But then I'd have to kill you."

Ben Hogan was as meticulous in his appearance as he was in his course management. He couldn't begin to understand players who grew their hair long or were disheveled in their appearance in any way.

Tom Weiskopf, who held Hogan in the highest regard, appeared at one early-season tournament sporting a neatly trimmed beard and mustache. He entered the locker room and saw Hogan sitting with some other players.

"Hi, Ben," said Weiskopf, walking over to shake Hogan's hand. "It's good to see you."

"What is that on your face?" Hogan asked sternly.

The beard and mustache were gone the next day.

Ben Hogan has a subtle sense of humor. Sometimes it's extremely subtle. Once, when I was working on a profile of Hogan's protégé, Gardner Dickinson, I asked Hogan why he thought it was that so few successful playing professionals are able to make the transition and become great teachers. As always, there was a pause as Hogan considered the question.

"I wasn't aware that he was either," Hogan finally replied.

Several seconds went by as I tried to figure out how to carefully phrase my next question.

"I'm just kidding, of course," he added, with perfect timing.

In the later years of his career, Hogan ran headlong into what passed for the "counterculture of the '60s" on the Tour. Politically, players may have still been Goldwater Republicans but they grew their hair longer and wore clothes that were far removed from what Tommy Bolt described as "Ben Hogan Blue and Grays."

One such player was Ron Cerrudo, who, to his combination of anticipation and horror, found he was going to be paired with Hogan. As luck would have it, the two men met in the locker room prior to their round.

"Mr. Hogan, it's going to be an honor to play with you," Cerrudo said.

Hogan eyed Cerrudo suspiciously.

"Son, you hook the ball, don't you?" he asked.

"Yes, sir, Mr. Hogan," Cerrudo answered nervously.

"Well, that's good, because I like to fade the ball," Hogan said. "Let's pretend there's a line right down the middle of the fairway. You hit your drives to the left of that line and I'll hit mine to the right. That way we won't have to talk."

Cerrudo was left stunned and speechless—until Hogan broke into a deep laugh.

For many years, Hogan's equipment company would host a dinner for its sales force and the tour players who endorsed Hogan clubs and balls.

One year Hogan appeared on the dais in a disheveled state, his hair uncombed and his clothes a mess. The room fell into a stunned silence. After a few minutes, Hogan excused himself. As soon as he left, the room was abuzz with speculation. Had Hogan lost his mind?

No, as he proved a few minutes later when he returned neatly dressed and groomed.

"Gentlemen," he said. "Let me ask you a question: Which person would you rather do business with?"

Hogan was of an era when players would dress in coat and tie for dinner, so naturally when long hair and loud clothes came along in the '70s—even on the Tour—Hogan was more than a little dismayed.

One year at the annual champions dinner during the Colonial Invitational, Hogan rose from the head table to propose a toast:

"Ladies and gentlemen, I want you to look around at these great champions," he said. "All these men have one thing in common. They all have nice, clean haircuts."

Then, having made his point, he sat down.

For a long time, Hogan resisted the suggestions from his marketing people that they pay players to endorse Hogan equipment.

"We don't need players," he explained. "We have me."

In Hogan's prime, players earned their money from endorsements and exhibitions.

"I couldn't win enough money to stay on tour and provide the life I wanted for Valerie and myself," he explained. "I had to play a lot of exhibitions."

After every win in a major, Hogan would raise his appearance fees. This led to some grumbling among other players.

"I don't know why they're upset," Hogan said. "When my fees go up, so do theirs."

Early in his career, Hogan worked as an assistant professional at the Century Country Club outside New York City.

Today there's a framed letter from one of the members hanging on a wall in the pro shop. It reads, in part, "This is to introduce Ben Hogan from Fort Worth, Texas. He is a fine young man and I believe he might have a future in this game."

Yes, to put it mildly.

Ben Hogan always enjoyed a comfortable relationship with the press. They respected him and his desire for privacy. He respected their need to get their jobs done as well as possible. Still, he was not above giving them a jab every now and then.

Although he would readily agree to post-round interviews, the fact that so few writers actually went out on the course to follow the players was a constant source of wonder for him. Instead, they would wait for players to come to the pressroom to describe their round, hole by hole.

"You know, one day a deaf mute is going to win a tournament and you guys will be in a helluva fix," he once joked to a pressroom full of writers.

Although Hogan preferred medal play, he was a formidable competitor in match play events. Witness his two PGA Championship victories and his numerous Ryder Cup wins.

In the 1951 Ryder Cup at Pinehurst he came to the 10th hole 1-up over Charley Ward, but it looked as if the match would draw even when Hogan hooked his drive into the woods. Ward, safely in the fairway, watched as Hogan studied his options. Finally, Hogan took his pitching wedge and hit the ball through a small opening in the pines, advancing it forty yards up the fairway. From there he tore into a 2-wood, and watched as the ball bounded onto the green some sixty-feet from the hole. From there, he made the putt to win the hole over a stunned Ward.

"My God, what do you have to do to win a hole from this man?" Ward asked.

Few players—if any—ever thought their way around a golf course better than Ben Hogan. He was the supreme strategist, and naturally players would seek him out for advice prior to a championship.

One year, when the U.S. Open came to San Francisco's Olympic Club, a young player asked Hogan about the course. Hogan stressed that although there was just one fairway bunker on the course, the Olympic Club course placed a premium on accurate driving, particularly under U.S. Open conditions.

The player asked Hogan if the bunker came into play.

"No," said Hogan matter-of-factly. "You drive to the right of it."

Ben Hogan's powers of concentration were legendary. Once he was paired with George Fazio in a tournament. Fazio, a very stylish player, holed an approach shot for an eagle. When they finished their round, Hogan handed Fazio the scorecard he'd been keeping.

"Ben, you've got me down for a 4 on the 5th hole," said Fazio. "Don't you remember, I made a 2?"

"No, George, number 5 is a par 4," replied Hogan.

"That's right, Ben," said Fazio. "I holed my approach shot."

When the third member of their group confirmed it, Hogan changed the score and signed the card.

"I'm sorry, George," he said. "I honestly don't remember seeing you hit that shot."

Bobby Nichols was an outstanding high-school athlete as a kid growing up in Louisville, Kentucky. But on September 3, 1952, he was critically injured in a car crash. The accident left him unconscious for thirteen days, and he suffered a broken pelvis, a concussion, and internal and back injuries. On top of that, he was paralyzed from the waist down. Doctors didn't believe he'd ever walk again, much less play sports.

Nichols was hospitalized for ninety-six days, and during that time his plight came to the attention of Ben Hogan, who had been seriously injured in an automobile accident in 1949. Hogan wrote a series of encouraging letters to Nichols, urging him not to give up and to have faith.

Nichols's recovery was slow and painful, but eventually he became strong enough to win junior tournaments in Kentucky and win a golf scholarship at Texas A&M. He joined the Tour in 1960 and won eleven tournaments, including the 1964 PGA Championship. In 1962, he won the Ben Hogan Award from the Golf Writers of America, an award given to a player who returned to golf following an accident or illness.

Decades after his playing days were over, Ben Hogan remained an inspiration to new generations of golfers. When Curtis Strange successfully defended his U.S. Open title in 1989 at Oak Hill, he became the first player to do so since Hogan in 1951.

When Curtis entered the pressroom he put his acomplishment in perspective.

"Move over, Ben," he joked as he sat down.

THE INVERNESS CLUB

The Inverness Club in Toledo, Ohio, holds a special place in golf history—and not just because it has hosted four U.S. Opens, two PGA Championships, and a U.S. Amateur. Inverness's importance dates back to the 1920 U.S. Open.

Until that year, professional golfers in both Great Britain and the United States were treated as social inferiors— mere hired help brought in to help put on a show. It's hard to believe today, when pros are celebrities and, in many cases, multimillionaires several times over, that back then, professionals were often not even allowed to change their shoes in the locker room, much less eat in the clubhouse.

But all that changed at Inverness. The club members, many of whom were hardworking, self-made men of solid midwestern stock, were offended by the treatment they saw other clubs heap upon the likes of Walter Hagen, Johnny Farrell, Gene Sarazen, and Tommy Armour. When the players arrived for the Open, they were warmly welcomed into the clubhouse, and the old ways were gone forever.

In appreciation, the professionals took up a collection at the end of the Open and purchased a magnificent, eight-foot-high clock that still stands today in the foyer of the clubhouse. Attached to the clock is a brass plaque that reads:

God measures men by what they are
Not by what in wealth possess.
This vibrant message chimes afar
The voice of Inverness.

Nobody really knows who wrote those lines, but we do
know that it was Walter Hagen's idea to present the club
with the clock. That's not surprising, since Hagen's concept
of equality was so liberal that he once told Edward, Prince
of Wales, "Eddie, hold the pin."

IRELAND

I once had a limousine driver in Chicago who offered a unique version of golf history. His name was Desmond, and he was a native of Ireland who'd come to America during World War II to work on the Manhattan Project, the top-secret effort to develop the atomic bomb.

Desmond was in his seventies and could have passed for the twin brother of Barry Fitzgerald, the actor who played the matchmaker in the greatest movie ever made, *The Quiet Man*, which also featured the most beautiful actress who ever lived, Maureen O'Hara.

All that aside, Desmond was a treasure who didn't need the money but drove his limo simply because it gave him a chance to meet new people. Honestly. Anyway, his story went something like this:

"Well, I suppose being a golf writer and all, you think that the game began with the Scots. That's not true, at all. The Irish invented it, we did. Back in the days when the great kings ruled Ireland they established what we called 'Common Grounds' for the use of all the people, you know, for gardens and the like. Now, since we Irish are a naturally caring people one of the uses of these common grounds were as places where the least fortunate mentally among us could gather and amuse themselves without being a bother

66

to the rest of the people. I don't like to use the word *retarded* because God Himself wouldn't care for it, but let's just say they had a special grace from our Father and leave it at that.

"Anyway, one day it came to pass one of the elders in the village watched some of these people hitting stones around with sticks and thought it might be more fun for them if they had a goal to their hitting. So he dug a wee hole in the ground and then showed them how to hockey the stones into it.

"Well, of course this was a perfect game for them and it kept them occupied for hours on end. Now, about this time the Irish began doing a fair amount of commerce by sea, and one of their favorite ports was St. Andrews in Scotland. When Irish ships began arriving in that godforsaken place they demonstrated their game to the Scots as a joke, you see. Naturally, the damned fools took it seriously. It's like their Presbyterianism—that religion of theirs. Christly dour, it is.

"Of course, they did the same thing with bagpipes. We gave them something that produces the softest, most lilting music you ever heard and they turned it into the most dreadful screeching imaginable. They use it to march to war and that's all it's fit for, really. Well, that's the Scots for you. British once removed, they are."

That's Desmond's story, and he's sticking to it.

JOCKS

Ivan Lendl, the great tennis player, was a passionate golfer even during his playing days. It wasn't unusual to see him at his home course, The Stanwich Club in Greenwich, Connecticut, shortly after finishing a match in the U.S. Open in nearby New York City. When a bad back required him to give up competitive tennis, he began to play in celebrity golf tournaments. One of these, in Lake Tahoe, was televised by NBC Sports.

Commentator Roger Maltbie was covering Lendl's group and watched Lendl hit balls into the water five times in the course of his round.

"Well, grass never was his best surface," Maltbie quipped.

"The thing to remember is that 99 percent of the putts that you leave short don't go in."
>—Yogi Berra, to his pro-am partners

"It wasn't my fault, coach. Blame the guys in the four-some in front of me."
>—Ex–New York Giant Lawrence Taylor,
>when asked by Coach Bill Parcells
>why he was late for a practice

BOBBY JONES

Very often, players who dominate an era meet with resentment and envy from their fellow players. Perhaps that is only human nature. Still, it speaks volumes for Bob Jones's character and sportsmanship that he was universally beloved by his fellow players—something perhaps all the more remarkable since he was an amateur outplaying the best professionals of his time and, in the case of players like Gene Sarazen and Walter Hagen, some of the best of all time.

Make no mistake, he was a fearsome competitor. It wasn't unusual for him to lose as much as fifteen pounds from stress in a Major championship. But like Jack Nicklaus today, he was even more gracious in defeat than he was magnanimous in victory.

When people look at sports today, and see strikes and drug abuse and cheating and all the other assorted scandals that take up all too much room in the sports pages, they are often struck by the sportsmanship that is so much a part of golf, on both the professional and amateur levels. That is in no small part the legacy of Bobby Jones. His example inspired not only players of his era, but players like Arnold Palmer, Jack Nicklaus, Ben Crenshaw and others. Their examples, in turn, inspire players who weren't even born when Bobby Jones died in 1971.

Early in his career, Bobby Jones was paired with Harry Vardon. The young Jones was understandably nervous and played badly. Vardon gave him a piece of advice: "Don't give up. Just keep hitting it. Something good might come of it." It was advice Jones never forgot.

Jones was once asked if there was ever a player he wanted to beat because he personally disliked the man. Jones wouldn't name the player but allowed that there was one.

"He came up to me before the final round of a championship," Jones told a close friend. "He told me that he really didn't care which one of us won, that he just wanted to have a pleasant round and he hoped the best man would win. I didn't like that. I knew he wanted to win very badly—just as much as I did—and he wasn't being honest with me. I wanted to beat him very badly from that moment on."

And no doubt he did.

One day Jones was scheduled to tee off at noon in oppressively hot weather. As he was leaving the locker room he asked a friend what the temperature was.

"A hundred and two in the shade, Bob," the man replied.

"Well, I'm glad we don't have to play in the shade," Jones joked.

Jones was deeply loved and respected by the people of the British Isles, a feeling reciprocated by Jones. After winning the 1927 British Open at St. Andrews, he addressed the large crowd that gathered in front of the old clubhouse. He told them that by winning the Open at St. Andrews he had fulfilled a lifelong ambition. He thanked them for their kindness during the championship. And then he told them that instead of taking the trophy back with him to America, he would leave it in the care and safekeeping of the R & A in St. Andrews.

The gallery roared with approval and appreciation.

With the possible exception of the galleries at the Masters, there are no galleries to equal those at St. Andrews. They are knowledgable and respectful, as Bob Jones's son discovered the first time he played the Old Course.

A large gallery turned out to see how their beloved Bobby's son would fare. Young Bob hit a good drive and had just a short wedge shot onto the first green. Sadly, he shanked the ball into the Swilken Burn. When he dared to look up, he saw the gallery quietly walking away. Upon his return home he told his father what had happened.

"The galleries at St. Andrews expect excellence, but they will not stand by and gawk at a painful death," his father explained gently.

In the 1930 British Amateur at St. Andrews, Jones met a Walker Cup teammate, George Voight, in the semifinals. Jones, under intense pressure as the favorite to win the championship, did something he'd never done before in tournament play: during the lunch break prior to his match, he decided to have a glass of sherry in the hope that it would settle his nerves.

Jones, who liked a drink as much as the next man, experienced an intense reaction to the alcohol. His vision became blurred. His balance was thrown off and he struggled to hang on and avoid defeat, but with five holes remaining he was two down to Voight—the only time in the championship he was more than one down to an opponent—and his chances of winning were looking slim.

But luck was with him. On 14, Voight drove the ball out of bounds and Jones narrowed the gap. On 18, with the match all square, Voight three-putted and Jones escaped to go on and win the next day. By the year's end, he had won both the British and U.S. Opens and Amateurs and retired from competitive golf.

Perhaps no player is more closely associated with St. Andrews than Bob Jones. He won both the British Open and Amateur there and, upon his retirement from competitive golf, returned unannounced for a quiet round with friends that resulted in the entire town turning out to watch him play the Old Course one last time.

Like many players, Jones did not love the Old Course at first sight. In fact, his first visit—in the 1921 Open—

resulted in a most uncharacteristic display of temper. Playing poorly in the third round, he took a 6 on the par-3 11th and tore up his scorecard in disgust.

But in time he came to understand the intricacies of the course and its considerable charm, as he explained when he returned to St. Andrews to be named an Honorary Burgess of the city—the first American to receive the honor since Benjamin Franklin.

"The more I studied the Old Course the more I loved it, and the more I loved it the more I studied it, so that I came to feel that it was for me the most favorable meeting ground possible for an important contest. I felt that my knowledge of the course enabled me to play it with patience and restraint until she might exact her toll from my adversary, who might treat her with less respect and understanding."

Bob Jones dueled with Al Watrous in the final round of the 1926 British Open at Royal Lytham and St. Annes. Tied coming to the 413-yard, par-4 17th hole, Watrous drove safely into the fairway and hit the green in two. Jones drove into a fairway bunker and faced a shot of 175 yards to a heavily bunkered green. Jones studied his options as the enormous gallery surged around him. Finally, he pulled a mashie (4-iron), lofted the ball up quickly over the lip of the bunker, and watched as it came to rest inside of Watrous's ball.

"There goes a hundred thousand bucks," Watrous said to his caddie while the ball was still in the air. Moments later—not surprisingly, perhaps—Watrous three-putted to lose the Open.

"An eighth of an inch too deep with the blade, off dry sand, and the shot expires right before your eyes," Jones later wrote. "And if your blade is a thought too high . . . I will dismiss this harrowing reflection."

Jones had a wonderful sense of humor and enjoyed playing jokes on his friends. One day he was playing an exhibition with Walter Hagen. When Hagen hit his ball into a bunker, Jones discreetly took a $20 bill from his pocket, rolled it into a ball, and tossed it into the sand near Hagen's ball. Naturally, when Hagen saw the bill he picked it up . . . and then laughed with the gallery as Jones called a penalty on him for removing a loose impediment.

Bob Jones suffered from syringomyelia, a degenerative nerve disease that is especially cruel since the body degenerates while the mind remains perfectly intact. As the time of his death approached, his body had wasted away to under a hundred pounds. He was bedridden and in considerable pain. Still, the courage he had displayed throughout his life was there until the end.

A few days before he died, his family gathered at his bedside.

"If this is all there is to dying, it's not so bad," he told them. "It's very peaceful."

When he heard of Jones's death, Ben Hogan issued a statement that was eloquent in its brevity.

"Bob Jones was sick for so long, and in fighting so hard to live he revealed his greatest strength to us. It was his strength of mind."

In 1958, Bob Jones traveled to St. Andrews to be presented with the Freedom of the Burgh. In the course of his remarks, Jones spoke movingly about friendship and his feelings about the people of St. Andrews. His words spoke volumes about the man himself:

"Friends are a man's priceless treasures, and a life rich in friendship is full indeed. When I say, with due regard for the meaning of the word, that I am your friend, I have pledged to you the ultimate in loyalty and devotion. In some respects, friendship may even transcend love, for in a true friendship there is no place for jealousy. When, without more, I say that you are my friends, it is possible that I am imposing upon you a greater burden than you are willing to assume. But when you have made me aware on countless occasions that you have a kindly feeling toward me, and when you have honored me by every means at your command, then when I call you friend, I am at once affirming my high regard and affection for you and declaring my complete faith in you and trust in the sincerity of your expressions."

When Jones died on December 18, 1971, word spread quickly around the golf world. At St. Andrews, players quit their rounds and silently walked off the course in Jones's honor.

TOM KITE

For many years, Tom Kite carried the label "the best player who never won a Major." That changed in 1992, when he won the U.S. Open at Pebble Beach with one of the finest last rounds in Open history.

A year or so later, a friend was in a clothing store and he saw a necktie with the image of Kite's swing on it.

"It's a funny thing," said Kite when he saw the tie. "It used to be that I couldn't get anyone to even look at my swing. Then I won the Open and people are putting it on neckties."

In the early 1990s, the members at Austin Country Club in Texas decided to commission a life-size bronze sculpture of the club's longtime professional, Harvey Penick, and one of his favorite pupils, Tom Kite.

When they approached Mr. Penick for his permission, he demurred, saying, "I've never done anything to deserve a statue."

When they approached Tom Kite, his reply was equally simple and to the point.

"I've never done anything to deserve being in a statue with Mr. Penick."

Nevertheless, the statue was erected on a spot near the clubhouse overlooking the golf course. Sadly, Mr. Penick couldn't attend the unveiling. Already quite frail, he was taken seriously ill and hovered near death, coming perilously close the evening before the ceremony.

"I can't die tonight," he said softly to his wife, Helen. "I want that ceremony to be joyous, not mournful."

Somehow, he held on that night and the next day until after the ceremony. Then he slipped quietly away from the people and the game he loved so deeply, and to whom he gave so much.

During the unveiling, Tom Kite fought back tears when he recalled being asked what was the best break he ever got in golf. He said it was when the Internal Revenue Service transferred his father from Dallas to Austin when Tom was thirteen years old.

"That's when I met Mr. Penick and Ben Crenshaw," he explained. "Even in my wildest dreams I couldn't have imagined a finer teacher or stronger competition."

Over the years, much has been made of the rivalry between Tom Kite and Ben Crenshaw and indeed, they have been competing against each other for more than thirty years—as juniors, teammates at the University of Texas, and on tour.

Still, for all their competition one of the things that moved Tom Kite the most following his win in the 1992 U.S. Open was something very simple: a letter of congratulations from Ben Crenshaw.

KY LAFFOON

Ky Laffoon was a fine player who won, among other tournaments, the inaugural Phoenix Open in 1935. For all his talent, though, he was best known for his temper, as Sam Snead remembers:

"When Ky would get mad he'd drop whatever club he was holding and begin punching himself in the head," says Sam. "One day he missed a putt and forgot to drop his putter. He hit himself on the head and knocked himself out."

TOM LEHMAN

Tom Lehman has become one of the top players on the PGA Tour in recent years. His singles match with Seve Ballesteros in the 1995 Ryder Cup was one of the highlights of the matches.

But for all his recent success, he struggled in his early years as a professional. At one point he considered taking a job as the pro at his alma mater, the University of Minnesota. The deal fell apart when he learned that he had to spend his winters renting cross-country skis out of the pro shop.

NANCY LOPEZ

Like many talented young players, Nancy Lopez was known to throw a club or two when she hit a poor shot. Her father, Domingo, quickly put a stop to this the first time he saw her fire a club into the air.

"It was one of those things that he just wouldn't tolerate," she recalls. "He told me if he ever saw me throw another club he'd pull me right off the golf course—and he would have, too."

After achieving stardom on the LPGA Tour, Nancy Lopez married Ray Knight, who had been an exceptional infielder with the Cincinnati Reds, the New York Mets, and the Baltimore Orioles. Like many successful athletes, he was fascinated by golf but not always patient when the game got the better of him.

One day Nancy and Ray were playing golf with Domingo. They came to a long par 5, and Ray tried to hit a particularly big drive. It didn't work out at all. And Nancy knew what was coming next.

"Ray, please don't throw that club," she pleaded.

No chance. Knight launched the club into the air.

"Nancy, you get in this cart right now," Domingo said firmly. "We're heading in."

Naturally, this posed a tremendous dilemma for Nancy.

Do you obey your father, to whom you're tremendously devoted and who you know is right? Or do you stay with your husband, who was wrong but still your husband?

She got into the cart and off they went.

"Ray was pretty mad, but he got over it," she said. "He knew my dad was right."

Nancy Lopez has always been quick to credit her parents for her success. Her father taught her how to play, and both parents sacrificed so she could play in tournaments as a kid. Her bond with her father became particularly close after her mother's death.

In her early years on tour, her father was a familiar figure at tournaments. Just as she did as a youngster, when she needed help with her game she turned to her father for advice. Far more often than not, it was the right advice.

As he got older, he traveled to fewer and fewer tournaments, but father and daughter would talk often over the phone. At one point, he became seriously ill, and she constantly worried about him.

One day he called her and said he had something he needed to tell her. Fearing the worst, she steeled herself for what was coming.

"Nancy, I watched you on television last weekend," he told her. "You're missing too many five- and six-footers."

DAVIS LOVE, JR.

Davis Love, Jr., the father of PGA Tour star Davis Love III, was one of America's top teaching professionals before he died in a plane crash in 1988. He had the wisdom and patience to work with poor players, but at the same time he had the playing experience that made him a valuable teacher for even the best players in the game—many of whom traveled to Sea Island resort for lessons and advice. He was by nature a quiet, gentle man, but he also had a fine sense of humor.

Davis taught for many years in the Golf Digest Schools and was every bit as highly regarded as Bob Toski, Peter Kostis, Jim Flick, or any of the other top teachers. For much of that time the schools were run by an administrator named Paul Menneg, who, it can be fairly said, had a healthy respect for a dollar.

One time Davis sent in an expense report that included the cost of an umbrella. Menneg sent it back to Davis saying that the schools wouldn't pay for such an extravagance. Davis was incredulous and appealed to Menneg, to no avail.

A few days later Davis sent in a revised expense report with a note: "Paul, there's an umbrella in here someplace. See if you can find it."

Davis, born and raised in the South, often was amused or even baffled by life in places like New York City.

One year he and several of his fellow teachers came to New York for some meetings. They had a day to kill, so they decided to go out to Long Island and play a couple of the great courses in the Hamptons. What they hadn't counted on was the huge traffic jam backing up at the bridge they would take off the island. They got into one of the exact-change toll lanes and resumed talking about the courses they had seen that day. When the time came to pay their toll, they realized that the smallest bill they had was a $20.

Now, bear in mind that it was hot and humid and that New Yorkers are not patient under the best of circumstances. It wasn't long before people began blowing their horns and yelling at the courtly southern gentleman walking from car to car looking for change for a $20.

Davis Love, Jr., enjoyed some success on tour, but in his heart of hearts he always wanted to be a teaching pro, like his mentor Harvey Penick.

As his two boys, Davis and Mark, grew older they both enjoyed the game, and it soon became obvious that young Davis had all the makings of a champion. To make sure the boy stayed on track, his father established a simple rule: when a decision had to be made about Davis's development as a player there would be three votes. Early on, his father would hold all three. As Davis became older and more experienced, he'd get one vote to his father's two. By the time he was in college and was one of the nation's top amateurs, he'd get two of the three. When he was ready to turn pro, he'd get all the votes.

And just to be on the safe side, his father arranged for Tom Kite to take young Davis under his wing on tour.

GEORGE LOW

George Low, who died in April 1995, was one of the legendary hang-around guys in golf. Dan Jenkins called him "America's Guest," and Low never saw any reason to disagree.

Low could usually be found in or near the clubhouse at a tournament, leisurely taking in whatever was going on around him. It was usually a good bet that a drink and a cigarette were not far away.

"George was born retired," the late Jimmy Demaret once said.

When Low wasn't at a tournament, he could usually be found at the home of a friend—usually a wealthy friend.

"I tend to favor places where a rich guy's got an extra bed and a kind heart," he used to say.

"I wish I just had your energy," Billy Maxwell once told Low as Low lounged around the clubhouse during a tournament.

"I wish I had a rock in each hand," Low replied.

When Low was diagnosed with cancer in 1994, doctors told him he had only six months to live.

"I'm playing extra holes," he told a friend.

Low was cremated. His ashes were buried at Cog Hill, the sprawling public golf facility outside Chicago.

At one tournament in the 1940s, Toney Penna checked into a hotel that was run by a friend of his. When he got to his room there was a large supply of free whiskey.

Word of Penna's good fortune soon spread, and it wasn't long before George Low and a friend showed up at Penna's door. Naturally, Penna denied knowing anything about any free booze. And naturally, Low and his friend didn't believe him.

The more Penna denied he had anything stashed away, the more convinced Low was that he was lying, and to find out Low and his friend took desperate actions. They opened a window, grabbed Penna, and hung him out the window some twenty stories above the street.

"It's in the trunk!" Penna yelled. When they had brought Penna back in, all three men sat down to some serious drinking.

MICKEY MANTLE

The Yankee great Mickey Mantle loved golf but was hobbled by the leg injuries he suffered in his baseball career. He liked the competition and the camaraderie, particularly when he played in celebrity pro-ams, which gave him a chance to visit with friends.

The Mick used to hold a tournament of his own in Georgia to raise funds for underprivileged kids. A photographer would wait at the 17th tee to take pictures of the groups as they came through. Mantle would arrange for his old teammate, Hank Bauer, to stand off to the side with a rubber snake rigged to a fishing rod. As each group lined up for their photo, Bauer would reel the snake near the group and Mickey would yell, "Snake!"

The prank scared former Baltimore Colt Tom Matte so badly that he jumped up on an expensive luxury car parked near the tee—spikes and all.

DAVE MARR

Over the years, people have struggled to come up with a set of criteria to define greatness in a golf course. Dave Marr's answer is not only the simplest but the best:

"If you'd tell your friend to get off the interstate and go play it, then it's a great golf course."

MERION GOLF CLUB

In 1960, the members at Merion Golf Club decided to commemorate one of the most historic moments in golf history: Bobby Jones's 8 and 7 win over Gene Homans in the finals of the 1930 U.S. Amateur. With this win, Jones completed his "Grand Slam"—winning the U.S. and British Opens and both nation's Amateurs. Following his win at Merion at age twenty-eight, Jones retired from championship competition.

To mark the event, the members arranged to have a plaque set on a large stone near the 11th tee—the hole where Jones closed out his match. Everything went fine, until somebody noticed that the marker read "Robert Trent Jones" instead of "Robert Tyre Jones." And although Trent Jones, the noted golf course architect, is certainly worthy of a plaque of his own, that wasn't what the members at Merion had in mind.

So, thinking quickly, they came up with a solution: a strip containing the correct name was placed over the plaque—which only proves that you can edit history.

Every year the members honor Jones and the Grand Slam with a quiet and moving celebration. Dressed in black tie, they walk from the clubhouse down to the 11th green. There, they drink a champagne toast to the man many believe was the greatest golfer in history.

Merion places a premium on accurate driving, although it's really not as difficult as Tommy Armour found it in the 1934 U.S. Open. He drove the ball out of bounds on the 420-yard, par-4 6th hole in all four rounds.

In the same Open, Bobby Cruickshank hit his approach to the 11th hole fat, and then watched with relief as the ball bounced off some rocks in the brook that guards the green. In his excitement, he tossed his club into the air, only to have it land on his head.

"It's the only time I've made a par by hitting two rocks on the same hole," he said.

The 18th hole at Merion is immortalized by Hy Peskin's classic photograph of Ben Hogan watching his approach shot fly toward the green in the fourth round of the 1950 U.S. Open.

The hole requires a drive through a chute of trees. A ball that lands short of the fairway will wind up in thick brush and scrub and will likely be unplayable—assuming you can even find it.

One year Paul Runyan, a two-time PGA champion, came to the 18th with a strong wind blowing into his face. Runyan thought it over, pulled out a wedge and pitched down to a forward set of tees, and then hit a fairway wood into play. The ploy left him with just a short iron to the green, and Runyan, who was brilliant from 100 yards in, made his par.

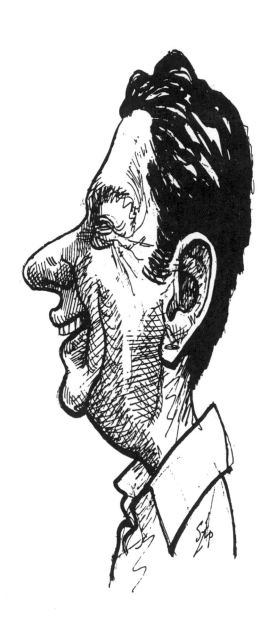

DR. CARY MIDDLECOFF

Doc Middlecoff is a wonder, really. He had a fine amateur career, and agreed to become a dentist only because his father had doubts about his son's ability to make a proper living as a touring professional. In the 1940s, when Doc turned pro, that was a legitimate concern, not because of Doc's talent, but because of the economics of tour life.

But Middlecoff would go on to have a wonderful career. He won thirty-nine Tour events, including two U.S. Opens and a Masters. He was one of the first players to successfully make the move into television, and worked for CBS Sports for many years.

He played in a couple of the early "Legends of Golf" tournaments, but his heart was never really in it. He once marveled at Sam Snead's enthusiasm for senior events, noting that "I really couldn't have cared less. For me, it was just a good chance to see some of my old friends. For Sam, it was like being a kid with his first set of clubs."

Indeed, no one was ever better than Doc Middlecoff when it came time to sit around and tell golf stories. In the late 1970s and into the 1980s, *Golf Digest* would arrange annual meetings of a select group of teachers and players. These included people like Sam Snead, Paul Runyan, Bob Toski, Peter Kostis, Davis Love, Jr., Jim Flick, Jack Lumpkin, and, of course, Doc Middlecoff. This panel would sit for hours and discuss every aspect of the game. The meetings would be followed by golf, dinner, and then after-dinner drinks and storytelling that went on well into the night. It's unlikely there will ever be another group that brought so much knowledge, experience, camaraderie, and love of the game to one place. And Doc was a big reason it all worked so well.

"People talk about the great rounds of golf, but no one ever mentions Jimmy Demaret's first round in the 1952 Crosby," Doc began in one of those late-night sessions. "He shot a 74 under conditions that were just unplayable. Period. He might have been the best wind player I ever saw. The harder it blew, the better he played. It just rained all day and it was bitterly cold. Chunks of ice were being blown down the fairways. I was playing at Cypress Point, and by the time I reached the 16th green I'd had enough. My four-some marked our balls and headed in. Along the way I met Peter Hay, the pro at Pebble Beach. He was a Scot and a real stickler on the rules. I told him the wind was blowing so hard that I couldn't get the ball to stay on the tee. He just sort of glared at me and said, 'Show me where it says in the rule book that the ball has to be played from a tee.'

"Anyway, there was a big conference between Bing and some of the rules officials about whether the round should be called off," Doc continued. "They finally decided we had to go back out. We got back out on Cypress, and just as I was about to play a shot, this really powerful gust tore off the ocean. I turned away, and out of the corner of my eye I caught a glimpse of the old western actor Grant Withers.

He was actually hanging on to a tree as the wind tore his rain suit off him.

"I ran into Jimmy later at Pebble Beach and we were trading horror stories," Doc said. "He told me that when he played 17 at Cypress—which is usually a drive and a short iron—the wind was so bad he had to hit a driver, a fairway wood, and a 4-iron. He one-putted for a par and said it was the greatest par of his life."

"Doc was great to me when I came out on tour, and so I really had mixed emotions when CBS offered me Doc's job as an analyst," remembers Ken Venturi. "I told them I wanted to talk to Doc before I agreed to take the job. I called Doc at his hotel and asked if I could come up and see him. When I got there I told him that CBS had offered me the job but I wanted him to hear it from me first. He was great about it. He told me that he'd heard that I was going to get the job, but he appreciated the fact that I'd come to him first. After that we sat around and had a few martinis. Doc always made the best martinis."

MUIRFIELD

There really isn't anything in American private clubs to compare with the secretary at a British club. They exist as lord and master of all they survey at the club. Very little goes on that escapes their notice, or occurs without their approval.

One of the most widely feared—or respected, depending on your feelings toward authority figures—secretaries was the autocratic Colonel Brian Evans-Lombe, a former cavalry officer in the British Army who reigned over Muirfield—the home of the Honourable Company of Edinburgh Golfers—from the late 1940s until the early 1960s.

Course conditioning was never a consuming passion in the British Isles until relatively recently, when some of the great old courses installed watering systems, much to the dismay of purists. But Evans-Lombe disagreed, and under his direction Muirfield became one of the first of the great clubs in the United Kingdom to place an emphasis on how its course looked, as well as how it played.

Armed with a powerful set of binoculars, Evans-Lombe would spend his free moments scanning across the course. Heaven help the poor player—especially a visitor and even more especially a tourist from the States—who neglected to replace a divot. Evans-Lombe was even known to berate a player who failed to replace a divot so that the grain was placed in the right direction.

At least you can say this about Colonel Evans-Lombe: he didn't play favorites. In 1959, the United States team traveled to Muirfield for the Walker Cup matches against the team from Great Britain and Ireland.

It should be noted here that for purists, the Walker Cup holds a special—and justifiable—significance. First of all, it is amateur golf at its highest level, unsullied by any hints of commercialism. Second, it celebrates the "Special Relationship" between the Americans and our British and Irish cousins. That may seem a quaint and outdated concept in this time of the global village, but it still holds true in golf, and the Walker Cup—with its memories of Bob Jones and Francis Ouimet, Bill Campbell and Jay Sigel, and so many others—still has a powerful pull on a segment of the golf world.

So you can only imagine the reaction when the president of the U.S. Golf Association, John Ames, dared to intrude upon Colonel Evans-Lombe in his private sanctuary at Muirfield on the eve of the matches.

Ames knocked on the door to the secretary's office, wishing only to introduce himself.

"Who's there and what is your business?" demanded Evans-Lombe.

Ames introduced himself and politely inquired if it might be too much to ask if he could have a locker.

BYRON NELSON

In 1945, Byron Nelson did something no golfer had ever done before and almost certainly will never do again: he won eighteen tournaments in one season, eleven of them in a row. The closest any player has come to matching this astonishing feat came in 1952, when Jackie Burke, Jr., won four in a row.

Nelson, who won fifty-two Tour events in a career that basically lasted just eleven years, is one of the most respected and beloved players in the history of the game. In 1995, on the fiftieth anniversary of his most remarkable season, much of the golf world paused to honor the man who, by anyone's standards, would rank as one of the five greatest players of all time.

In February of that year, a dinner was held in Orlando to commemorate Nelson's Streak and to honor him for his lifetime of remarkable accomplishments. Sam Snead, who along with Ben Hogan was born the same year Byron Nelson was, spoke at the dinner.

"Byron was a fierce competitor," said Sam. "He'd play you right to the hilt. You know, Byron would never drink or smoke or go out at night with the other fellas. All he wanted to do was play golf. He didn't care about having fun."

When it was his turn to speak, Byron showed that on top of his other talents, he also has a finely tuned sense of humor.

"I don't know about you, Sam, but winning eighteen tournaments in one year was sure a lot of fun for me," said Byron.

Byron Nelson has led an exemplary life. A devoutly religious man, he has always stressed that people in the public eye, especially athletes, have a responsibility to set a good example. That's why, when asked if he ever did anything he regrets, he points to a decision he made in 1936 that bothers him to this day.

"I was approached by a cigarette manufacturer who offered me $500 to endorse a brand called 20 Grand," he recalls. "Now, of course, that was quite a bit of money in those days, and I didn't think it through. I didn't realize the consequences and how many people something like that could influence, so I agreed to endorse the cigarettes, even though I never smoked. Well, as soon as those ads appeared I started to get the most painful letters from teachers and Sunday-school teachers asking me how I could do something so terrible. I must have gotten five hundred or more letters, all asking me why I would stoop so low just to chase the almighty dollar. And they were right, of course.

"Well, I just felt terrible about the whole thing, and I went to the company and tried to give them their money back if they would just cancel the ads," he went on. "They wouldn't and I still regret it. I've prayed about it often and I made a promise to the Good Lord, and said that for as long as I lived I'd never again do anything to influence people in the wrong way."

It's a promise Byron Nelson has kept for almost sixty years.

JACK NICKLAUS

It's often been said that as magnanimous as Jack Nicklaus is in victory, he's even more impressive in defeat. That's certainly true. But it's also true that as impressive as he is in the public arena, he's also a sportsman of the first order away from the course. Here are a couple of examples.

As you might expect, Jack Nicklaus is hugely popular in Japan and has traveled there frequently throughout his career. On one such trip, he met with the Prime Minister and the United States Ambassador. When he returned to his hotel, he arranged for room service so he could get some work done with his business associates.

When the room service arrived, one of the waiters politely requested an autograph. Not only did Nicklaus give the man his autograph, he spoke with him for a good twenty minutes, asking him about his family, his golf game, and so on. When the waiter left, one of Nicklaus's friends asked why he had spent as much time with a waiter as he did with the Prime Minister.

"Why not?" Nicklaus replied. "They both treated me the same."

On another trip to Japan, Nicklaus had his putter stolen. This, of course, was treated as a national scandal and received widespread publicity—which was heightened when it was revealed that the thief was none other than the son of one of Japan's leading newspaper editors.

"I hope the boy's life isn't ruined by forty-five seconds of foolishness," Nicklaus said, trying to deflect some of the pressure from the young man.

In an attempt to make a sort of national amends, the Prime Minister requested a meeting with Nicklaus to personally return the stolen club.

"I don't think that's a good idea," said Nicklaus. "Why doesn't someone just quietly slide it under the door and we'll be done with it?"

Golfers take great pride in the fact that they are their own rules officials. Of course, that's not to say that there haven't been players—even some top players—who have been known to skirt the rules.

One year at the Westchester Classic, Jack Nicklaus was paired in the first round with a player who consistently marked his ball and then replaced it in a slightly different position in order to take spike marks out of play.

Nicklaus didn't say anything to the man during the round, but after they had signed the scorecard Nicklaus pulled him aside.

"We're going to be paired together tomorrow, and I want you to know one thing," Jack said. "Every time you mark your ball you're going to see a pair of white shoes nearby. They'll be mine."

The man got the message.

Jack Nicklaus has always been meticulous about preparing for a tournament, and that includes having an encyclopedic knowledge of the rules—in fact, he reads the rules of golf in their entirety at the start of each year.

This all proved beneficial one year at the Masters when his ball came to rest against a peanut shell. Nicklaus called for a rules official and requested relief, which the official denied, arguing that a peanut is a natural—as opposed to an artificial—impediment.

"But it's a roasted peanut," Jack protested, "so it is artificial."

Jack got a drop.

As a young man, Nicklaus was a tremendously powerful player. He could overpower a course much as John Daly does today.

One year he was playing in the Tournament of Champions at La Costa. On the 16th tee he decided to try and hit an extra-long drive. After he hit the ball the club's shaft slammed against his back and broke in two with a loud crack.

Nicklaus turned around sharply, thinking that somebody had come out of the gallery and hit him on the back.

Jack Nicklaus was giving an exhibition on Paradise Island in the Bahamas many years ago. As he stood on the tee, hitting 2-iron shots out into the ocean, a member of the gallery issued a challenge: Off in the distance was a series of lights strung along a wire. Each light was covered by a paper globe. The man asked Nicklaus if he thought he could hit one of the paper globes with a golf ball.

Nicklaus studied the shot, walked into position, and fired a 2-iron shot at the lights. He didn't hit a light. He hit the wire instead.

Jack Nicklaus was playing with some business associates at the Lost Tree Club in Florida. They came to the 18th hole, a dogleg left with a pond protecting the corner. Ordinarily, it was a pond that Nicklaus could easily carry, but on this day he hit his drive into the middle of the pond.

"That was either the worst hook you ever hit or the best customer golf you've ever played," said his partner as they left the tee.

It's doubtful that anyone ever prepared better for a tournament—especially a major championship—than Jack Nicklaus has throughout his career. That even goes for the clothes he wears.

"If I'm in position to win at Augusta, I make it a point to wear something that will go nicely with a Green Jacket," he once said.

Allan Turnbull is a fine golfer from Peebles, Scotland, a former member of both the Scottish Youths and International teams who once made it to the semifinals of the British Amateur. In 1987, he decided to try to qualify for the British Open at Muirfield. He drew North Berwick as a qualifying site, and was pleased when he learned that he had been paired with Jack Nicklaus, Jr., in the qualifying round.

Everything went fine until the first green. Turnbull had lined up his putt and settled over the ball. He looked up toward the hole and saw the Great Man—Jack Nicklaus, Sr.—tending the pin. It was too much for Turnbull. He backed away from the ball, pondered for a moment the notion that the man who had won twenty major championships was caddying in his group, and then tried to make the putt.

He didn't, and he didn't qualify either. Still, he will always regard it as one the most memorable rounds of golf he ever played.

Jack Nicklaus came to the 1994 U.S. Open at Oakmont without much real hope of winning. He was fifty-four years old, and his last win in a major had been the 1986 Masters—which was also his last win on the PGA Tour. Still, he had won his first Major and first Tour event at Oakmont in the 1962 U.S. Open, so few people were prepared to totally count him out, least of all his wife, Barbara.

Before the first round she looked him deep in the eyes and put a spell on him.

"You're twenty-two, you're twenty-two," she said.

He went out and shot a 69, which left him one shot behind the leader, Tom Watson. After a 70 in the second round he shot a third-round 77. A writer asked him what happened to Barbara's spell.

"I looked in the mirror," he laughed.

In 1962, Jack and Barbara Nicklaus had a birthday dinner with a friend, Johnny Swanson, at the Del Monte Lodge in Pebble Beach. The dinner was in full swing when Swanson told Nicklaus he had an important phone call in the lobby. When Nicklaus picked up the receiver, he heard a man's voice singing "Happy Birthday."

"Who is this?" Nicklaus asked sternly.

"This is Bing Crosby," said the voice on the other end of the call.

"Oh, sorry," said Nicklaus. "I didn't recognize the voice."

Jack Nicklaus and Arnold Palmer teamed together to represent the United States in the 1963 World Cup at Nom-La-Breteche in Paris. In the final round, Nicklaus birdied the 4th and 5th holes, but bunkered his approach to the 7th hole, leaving himself a long explosion shot of some seventy yards.

Nicklaus carefully studied the shot, and then hit it perfectly, watching as the ball rolled into the cup for his third straight birdie. As soon as the ball rolled into the cup there was a commotion in the gallery. A gentleman had gotten so excited that he fell off his shooting stick and landed on his back.

That gentleman was the Prince of Wales. It wasn't the first time he'd fallen down on the job, so to speak.

Jack Nicklaus reached the finals of the 1959 U.S. Amateur at the Broadmoor in Colorado Springs. His opponent was the defending champion, Charlie Coe, who was one of the best amateurs of his generation.

The two had a classic duel, and came to the final hole with the match squared. Nicklaus had an eight-footer for a birdie, while Coe had a long putt for his birdie. When Coe missed, he walked over to his ball and picked it up. He instantly realized that Nicklaus hadn't given him the putt and that technically he'd just lost the hole and the championship. He looked over to Nicklaus and offered to concede.

"No, Charlie, that's no way to win," said Nicklaus, who went on to make his putt for his first of two U.S. Amateur titles.

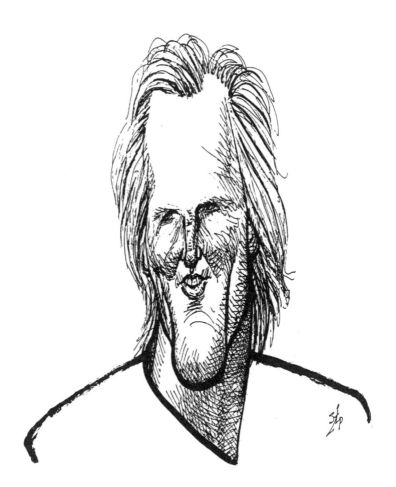

GREG NORMAN

Anyone who has kept track of Greg Norman's garage full of high-powered sports cars wouldn't be surprised to learn that he has long been fascinated with jet aircraft. In fact, that interest almost cost him a career in professional golf.

As a teenager, he trained for two years to become a fighter pilot in the Royal Australian Air Force. He had a natural aptitude for flying and passed every test that came his way, and the Air Force was quite anxious to have him commit to a five-year tour of duty.

He and his father went to Air Force headquarters to sign the necessary papers. As Norman and his father sat at a table with his squadron leader, Norman hesitated—pen in hand. He looked over at his father, who was beaming proudly. As he prepared to sign, a voice in his head kept saying, "Nope, don't do it. Don't sign. Go play golf."

Norman apologized and never looked back. No great loss, though. If he wanted to fly a Royal Australian Air Force fighter today, he could probably buy one.

MOE NORMAN

Canada's Moe Norman is an eccentric, if talented, player. Many people rank him with Sam Snead and Ben Hogan for the quality of his ball-striking. Although Norman enjoyed wonderful success in Canada, he never felt truly comfortable playing in America. Many people attributed this to an inferiority complex that manifested itself when he faced the Americans.

In 1956, Norman was invited to the Masters by virtue of his win in the Canadian Amateur. Admittedly nervous, he managed to make it through the first round, and then headed for the practice tee. There he ran into Sam Snead, whom he idolized. Sam watched him hit a few balls and then offered a couple of tips.

Norman, who was totally self-taught, was so flattered that he immediately began beating balls, trying to ingrain Sam's lesson. Unfortunately, he overdid it, hitting almost a thousand balls until his hands were raw and the skin on his left thumb had split.

The next day he tried to play, but had to quit after the second round. He boarded a bus and headed home to Canada, where he has lived in relative obscurity until recently, when he became the subject of numerous newspaper and magazine articles.

OAKMONT COUNTRY CLUB

The members at Oakmont pride themselves on their course's difficulty. And with good reason. The course is a killer, largely owing to the combination of deep rough, ferocious bunkering, and fast, undulating greens.

Actually, the course plays a little easier now because the bunkers are no longer raked in furrows two inches wide and two inches deep.

"If they could have made North Africa look like Oakmont's bunkers, Rommel wouldn't have gotten out of Casablanca," Jimmy Demaret once quipped.

And how dangerous were the greens? In the 1935 U.S. Open, Jimmy Thomson—then the longest hitter in the game—drove the 322-yard, par-4 17th. At the time he was tied for the lead with Sam Parks. Unfortunately for Thomson, when you reach the greens at Oakmont the fun is just beginning. He went ahead and four-putted. It could have been worse.

"When the ball got two feet from the hole I thought I had an eagle for sure," he told reporters. "Then it really took off. I had to make a three-footer just to save a bogey. Hell, on one of those holes I put down a dime to mark my ball. When I came back the dime had slid off the green."

MAC O'GRADY

It's doubtful anyone has endured more humiliation and disappointment when trying to earn a place on the PGA Tour than Mac O'Grady—or was more unhappy once he got there.

Beginning in 1971, he tried for ten years—through seventeen qualifying schools—to earn his playing card. The day he finally made it, he went out and bought sixteen baseball bats—one for each time he failed—and that night went out and smashed them all against a big tree.

THOMAS P. "TIP" O'NEILL

Tip O'Neill, the former Speaker of the House, was an avid golfer and the quintessential Irish-American.

One day he was at a golf tournament when a group of bagpipers began playing to mark the beginning of the tournament.

"You know, the Irish invented bagpipes and sent them to the Scots as a joke," he said to a friend. "Wouldn't you know, the fools took them seriously."

FRANCIS OUIMET

In 1963, the U.S. Open came to The Country Club in Brookline, Massachusetts, to celebrate the fiftieth anniversary of Francis Ouimet's Open victory over Harry Vardon and Ted Ray. A number of past Open champions attended a dinner honoring Ouimet. Among them were Walter Hagen, Johnny Farrell, Gene Sarazen, Julius Boros, Arnold Palmer, and Jack Nicklaus.

The speakers that night not only praised Ouimet's accomplishments as a player—which included a U.S. Open victory, two U.S. Amateurs, and membership on eight Walker Cup teams, including two that he captained. They also spoke about all that he gave back to the game. By the end of the evening, there was one more credit to add to that list: the Francis Ouimet Caddie Scholarship Fund, which got its start with the $40,000 raised at that dinner.

After his win over Vardon and Ray, somebody asked Ouimet whether he had spoken with the two Englishmen during the playoff.

"No," said the young Ouimet. "I was too afraid to speak to them, and the first time they spoke to me was to congratulate me on winning. Even then, I was too frightened to speak to them."

The members of The Country Club showed a graceful touch following Ouimet's win in the Open. Knowing the young amateur had limited funds, at best, they passed the hat to pay Ouimet's caddie, Eddie Lowery.

Francis Ouimet was also modest about his accomplishments. He was a friendly man by nature, and easy to approach.

Although he got his start in the sporting goods business, he soon gravitated to the world of finance; he worked for the investment firm of White, Weld in Boston. One afternoon, when Ouimet was in his seventies, he was at his desk when a repairman from the telephone company came to the office to do some work. Summoning all his nerve, the man shyly approached Mr. Ouimet's desk, nervously wiping his hands on his pants leg.

"Mr. Ouimet," he asked, "do you suppose I might shake your hand?"

Ouimet shook hands with the man and engaged him in a conversation about his own golf game. When the man left,

Ouimet mentioned the incident to the receptionist, and expressed his surprise that even at this stage in his life, people still knew who he was.

"When I pointed you out to him he stopped me," said the receptionist. "He said, 'Oh, I know which man is Mr. Ouimet. Everybody in Boston does.'"

ARNOLD PALMER

Arnold Palmer won the 1954 U.S. Amateur, which qualified him for an invitation to the Masters the following spring. When he arrived at Augusta National, Jackie Burke, Jr., asked the twenty-four-year old if he would like to join him and Ben Hogan for a practice round. Naturally, Palmer accepted the invitation, although he didn't exactly make an instant impression on Hogan.

On the first hole, Hogan hit the fairway and the green and made his par. Palmer hit his drive into the trees, scrambled around, and managed to sink a tough putt for his par. The next hole, a par 5, wasn't any better. Hogan hit the green in regulation and made his par. Palmer was in and out of the woods, and made another difficult putt to save par. Palmer hit another poor drive on the third hole, and as Hogan and Burke walked up the fairway to their balls, Hogan turned to Burke and asked a very logical question:

"How in hell did this guy get in the tournament?"

124

Palmer left Wake Forest following the death of his close friend, Buddy Worsham. Although he always wanted to become a pro, he was adrift and not sure where his life was headed.

One day he met a man from Cleveland who offered him a job selling trucks equipped with hydraulic lifts. He was willing to pay Palmer $50,000 for two years—an attractive figure for a young man back in the early 1950s. Tragically, the man was killed in an automobile accident before Palmer could sign the contract.

The next year Palmer won the U.S. Amateur and turned pro.

Palmer was long a fixture on the American Ryder Cup team, and one of his most memorable matches came in the 1961 competition at Royal Lytham and St. Annes. Going into the last day's singles matches, the U.S. team led, 6–2, and Palmer was matched against England's Peter Alliss in what figured to be the pivotal match.

Palmer's play was inspired, if not pretty. He holed from off the greens three times, and after seventeen holes the match was all square.

On 18, Alliss hit a poor drive and his second shot left him fifty yards short of the green. He pitched up to within a couple feet of the hole. Palmer gave Alliss his short putt, and then hit a mediocre approach putt of his own. As he prepared to hit his next putt, Alliss graciously went over and picked up Palmer's ball.

"We've had a great match, Arnold," he said. "Let's call it a halve."

Dave Marr was paired with Arnold Palmer in the first day's matches of the 1965 Ryder Cup at Royal Birkdale. It was a great pairing for Marr, who was playing in his only Ryder Cup, since Palmer was one of his best friends.

"I was on the first tee and I've never been so nervous on a golf course," Marr remembers. "Prime Minister Harold Wilson was there, which didn't exactly help. I mean, I was choking so bad I literally couldn't catch my breath. I was glad Arnold was driving on this hole. I don't think I could have gotten the ball onto the tee.

"Anyway, Arnold hit a great drive and all I had was a 5-iron left to the green. I must have hit six inches behind the ball. I laid the divot right over the ball. Arnold came over with this quizzical kind of look on his face and asked me if I'd had a bad lie. All I could do was admit I was choking like a dog. He laughed and then hit his shot stiff."

It's unlikely that there's ever been a player of Palmer's stature who has had more patience with either the fans or the press. No question is too stupid. Well, almost none.

Palmer was answering questions in a press conference one day when a writer asked him if he'd watched much golf on television as a boy.

"When I was a boy, they had just invented radio," he answered.

Palmer's enormous appeal certainly stems in part from his power and athleticism. His broad shoulders, huge arms, and narrow waist gave him a look much different from that of most other players of his era. It didn't hurt that when he came through the ropes onto a tee, he looked every bit like a fighter entering the ring. And it didn't hurt that he didn't so much swing at the ball as assault it, with a hugely powerful, slashing motion that sent the ball screaming off the clubface with a low, boring trajectory.

Palmer understood that part of his appeal, and went to lengths to ensure it wasn't diminished.

"We were filming the old 'Shell's Wonderful World of Golf' series on Eleuthera, which meant the players had the option of either playing the American ball or the smaller British ball," remembers Fred Raphael, the producer of the series. "Julius Boros chose the small ball, and was routinely outdriving Arnold, who was playing with the American ball. About halfway through the round, Arnold pulled Gene Sarazen, our commentator, aside and suggested that he explain to the viewers why he was being outdriven."

Arnold Palmer teamed with Jack Nicklaus in the 1963 World Cup matches at Nom-La-Breteche in Paris. For a time it appeared that Palmer might not be able to compete because of a thumb injury. Fortunately, Nicklaus's father, Charlie, had made the trip. As a pharmacist, he was able to suggest some medication that would ease the pain.

To Palmer's relief, the medication worked, and he opened with rounds of 66-67-67 and was well on his way to winning the individual title. After the third round, Charlie Nicklaus suggested it would be a good idea to stop taking the medication. Palmer did, but the next day he suffered a withdrawal.

He skied to a 78.

Palmer traveled to St. Andrews for the 1995 British Open; he had announced it would be his last British Open as a player. He did promise to come back for the fall meeting of the R & A.

"I'm playing like a member now, so I might as well play in their tournament," he joked.

When it became obvious that he wasn't going to make the cut, a huge gallery turned out to watch Palmer play up 18. Billy Andrade, who attended Wake Forest on an Arnold Palmer scholarship, lingered on his way down the first fairway and gave Palmer a thumbs-up. As Palmer crossed the ancient stone bridge over the Swilken Burn—which every great player in history except Ben Hogan has walked across—he paused and waved to the crowd, which roared its appreciation.

Even England's Nick Faldo came out of the clubhouse to honor Palmer, though he insisted he had another reason:

"I just wanted to see a Scotsman cry," he joked. "I couldn't find one."

PEBBLE BEACH

Peter Hay was a Scotsman who served for many years as the professional at Pebble Beach. He was a no-nonsense character with a deep, strong voice and a gruff manner. He also had some firm, simple ideas about how the game should be played.

"Play your shots quickly and don't complain," he advised people.

More's the pity that people don't play that way these days.

HARVEY PENICK

Harvey Penick was perhaps the most unlikely celebrity in golf. In 1991, he was suffering from a variety of illnesses ranging from prostate cancer to a debilitating case of arthritis. For much of his career—which was spent entirely at Austin (Texas) Country Club—he had seldom left Austin, let alone Texas. He was beloved by those who knew him and respected by those who knew his knowledge of the game and his devotion to teaching it.

But he recovered from the brink of death and decided to collaborate on a book based on a diary he had kept throughout his career. His *Little Red Book* went on to become the largest-selling sports book in history. He went on to write two more books with coauthor Bud Shrake, and was at work on a fourth when he died in April 1995 at age ninety.

Just a week before his death, when it was clear that he had little time left, he was visited by one of his longtime pupils, Ben Crenshaw, and Crenshaw's wife and two young daughters. Mr. Penick lapsed in and out of consciousness, until Ben mentioned that he'd been struggling with his putting. Suddenly, Penick was revived. In a strong, firm voice he ordered Crenshaw to go and get Penick's old, hickory-shafted Gene Sarazen putter. He watched Ben carefully and gave him some advice. Two weeks later, Crenshaw would win the Masters, crediting a fifteenth club in his bag—Harvey Penick.

A few days after the Crenshaws' visit, Penick was gripped by pneumonia and taken by ambulance to the hospital for the final time. En route, one of the attendants asked Mr. Penick to check his grip. He happily agreed.

The following Sunday, a bronze statue of Penick and Tom Kite was scheduled to be unveiled at Austin Country Club. Penick knew his time was short now, but he fought on, seemingly willing himself to live until the ceremony was over. When it ended, family and some close friends returned to the Penick home to gather around him. Death was near now, but he had one more player to bring home.

In New Orleans, Davis Love III was fighting for a win that was his last chance to get into the Masters the following week. His father had played for the University of Texas golf team that Penick coached and had been particularly close to Penick.

When Davis got into a playoff, Tom Kite gave the news to Penick. Unable to speak now, Mr. Penick softly clapped his hands together in joy. A few minutes later his son-in-law, Bill Powell, passed the word that Davis had won and was headed to the Masters.

Only then could Harvey Penick move on.

"Mr. Penick's in heaven watching the Masters with Bobby Jones," an emotional Ben Crenshaw said when he heard the news of Harvey Penick's death.

If so, Penick thoroughly enjoyed the tournament. Ben Crenshaw edged Davis Love III. Just like in the storybooks.

Harvey Penick was giving a lesson to a young man at the Austin Country Club. They stood on the practice tee and Mr. Penick asked his student to hit a few shots. The man hit one ball perfectly, and they watched as it rose off the clubface. Suddenly, the ball fell to the ground. The two walked down the range to see what had happened. A short distance away they found a bird that had been killed in flight by the ball.

"Darndest birdie I've ever seen," said Mr. Penick.

PINE VALLEY

Rankings of golf courses routinely list Pine Valley as one of the greatest courses in the United States—and with good reason. It is psychologically terrifying. The greens are frightening. The hazards are numerous. And then there are the trees, which are thick and unforgiving, as Laddie Lucas, a member of the 1936 Great Britain/Ireland Walker Cup team, discovered.

On one hole he hit a big slice off into the woods.

"Keep your eye on it!" he yelled to his caddie.

"You don't have to watch them here, sir," the caddie said. "Just listen for them."

POLITICIANS

In the years just before his death in 1995, Mickey Mantle organized a golf tournament in Georgia to help raise money for underprivileged kids. One year he looked down the entry list and saw that he was paired with Senator Sam Nunn.

"Who the hell is he?" The Mick asked.

"Only one of the most powerful people in Washington," a friend told him. "Be on your best behavior."

Everything went fine until Nunn—who is a fine golfer—holed a long birdie putt.

"You're a lucky son of a bitch," Mantle said, then quickly covered his mouth in embarrassment.

"You're right, I am a lucky son of a bitch," Nunn said, laughing.

THE PRESS

Bill Davis was selling commercial time for CBS in Chicago back in the early 1950s when he came up with an idea for a golf magazine. The game was growing in popularity in the postwar years, and Davis thought there might be a market for a magazine that catered to the expanding audience. He talked two friends, Howard Gill and Jack Barnett, into joining him and *Golf Digest* was born. Today it is the largest single-interest magazine in the world.

The magazine was sold to The New York Times Company, and Davis moved on to become a vice president with the *Times*, but he never lost his love for the magazine or for the game.

To say that Bill Davis was never a stereotypical, button-down corporate executive is to put it mildly. He was eccentric, provocative, occasionally volatile, and sometimes even outrageous. He could be scatterbrained, and often he'd come up with a great idea totally out of left field—and occasionally out of a deeply fogged left field. Still, he was a genius and an original and a passionate lover of the game.

It's not unusual for consumer magazines like *Golf Digest* to avoid offending advertisers, and Bill Davis had as healthy a respect for the bottom line as the next publisher. But he also had a simple belief that he repeated, mantra-like, to his editors.

"If you don't get somebody mad at you in each issue, you're not doing your job," he used to say.

It's fair to say that Bill Davis loved golf. It's also fair to say that he didn't exactly have a singular, Ben Hogan–like approach to the game. He'd take lessons from anyone. Scarcely a cocktail party went by that he didn't buttonhole someone for advice on his alignment—advice that sometimes wound up in *Golf Digest* but almost always failed to help its cofounder.

For many years, Bill Davis played in a company golf tournament open to all employees. It was a match play event that was played out over the course of the summer. Davis loved to participate in it because as the magazine grew, it gave him a chance to get to know new employees.

One year he was scheduled to play Steve Szurlej, the magazine's senior staff photographer. Davis invited Szurlej to play at one of his clubs, Millbrook, in the wealthy New York City suburb of Greenwich, Connecticut.

There were no caddies available when Davis and Szurlej arrived, so Szurlej decided to carry his bag, while Davis pulled a cart.

They teed off the first hole and headed down the fairway. As Szurlej walked ahead to his ball, he heard a crash, and looked back to see Davis picking up his bag. A few minutes later, he heard another crash and saw Davis again picking up his clubs. When it happened a third time, Szurlej went back to see what the problem was. It didn't take long to figure out.

"Bill," he said. "I think you've got to pull the wheels out away from the cart."

It's no secret that not everyone who gets credit for writing a book actually sits down and does the typing. Bill Davis was no exception.

One year he came up with the idea for a coffee table–size book based on *Golf Digest*'s ranking of the "100 Greatest Golf Courses in America." It was an inspired idea.

Davis walked into the office of one of the magazine's senior editors, Ross Goodner, and gave him the good news.

"Ross, I'm going to do a book based on the '100 Greatest' and you're going to write it for me," he said, scarcely able to contain his enthusiasm.

Goodner, who had known Davis for years, saw his life pass before his eyes.

Nevertheless, the book somehow got done and was an instant success. A few months after its publication, Davis was playing at the Garden City Golf Club just outside New York City with another of his editors.

"Gee, do you know who designed this course?" he asked the editor as they walked toward the third green. "I should know, but I haven't read that part of my book yet."

Television golf commentators are not always picked for their jobs because of their vast knowledge of the game's intricacies. In fact, many have only a passing knowledge of—or interest in—the game. Sometimes this becomes apparent to even the most casual viewer.

One year CBS Sports tried out a new announcer at the Masters, of all places. The announcer was assigned to the 14th hole, and things went smoothly enough until Sunday afternoon, when Seve Ballesteros came to the hole. Ballesteros hit a magnificent drive, leaving himself just 100 yards to the hole.

Seve studied the shot, pulled a wedge from his bag, and set up over the ball. Just as he was about to play his shot, he was distracted. He looked over at the gallery and said, "Fore, please."

The announcer spoke up.

"Seve has decided to change clubs," he whispered. "He's asked his caddie for a 4-iron."

Unlike writers, who have editors and erasers, announcers live or die with their words as they are spoken. Occasionally, they aren't always the best choice of words, as another announcer for CBS Sports learned at the Masters.

Nick Price had settled over his ball and was preparing to play, when he noticed that the wind had changed direction.

"There was a gust of wind from Nick's rear just as he was about to play," the announcer said.

No sooner had the words left his mouth than CBS's veteran producer/director Frank Chirkinian barked a question into the announcer's headset.

"Did Nick have Mexican food last night?"

Lesley Visser, who currently does on-air work for ABC and ESPN, got her start at the *Boston Globe* in the mid-1970s. She was one of the first women to break into the old-boys' clubs that were the sports departments of major American newspapers. In Lesley's case, it didn't hurt that she combined a graceful writing skill with a world-class personality and sense of humor.

One time she and a friend were in a bar when a drunk came along and tried to pick her up. After a few minutes, Lesley had heard about all she could stand.

"You sure know a lot about sports," he told her.

"I work for the *Globe*," she answered. "And what do you do?"

"I work for a company that grinds optical lenses," he said.

"Oh, that must be why you're making a spectacle out of yourself," she said.

Perfect.

In 1970, the unions for Britain's newspapers went on strike and the publishers refused to send writers over to cover the U.S. Open at Hazeltine. The only British writer at the tournament was Leonard Crawley, the legendary golf correspondent for London's *Daily Telegraph*.

This would have been seen as a shrewd move by the British publishers were it not for the fact that England's Tony Jacklin won the championship, becoming the first British subject to win the U.S. Open since Tommy Armour, who was born in Scotland, won in 1927.

As Crawley prepared to call his story in to London, he paused to gleefully savor his incredible good fortune.

"At this moment, gentlemen," he rejoiced, "all of England lies prostrate at my feet."

Early in his newspaper career, Crawley was sent to the English Boys' Championship. Upon his return he submitted an expense report that included £25 for entertaining some of the players. Naturally, the paper's accountants questioned the expense, figuring that the only person Crawley was entertaining was himself. Crawley protested.

"It's remarkable how much lemonade the little tykes can drink," he said.

Crawley was an accomplished sportsman, and quite a good golfer in his own right. He was a member of the 1932 Great Britain/Ireland Walker Cup team and played quite well at The Country Club just outside Boston. But going into the final day's singles match against George Voight, a box of matches exploded as he held them, burning his hands badly. Still, he insisted that he play, and going into the final hole of his match he was 1-up.

After hitting a good drive, he had a 5-iron left to the green. He hit a good shot, and watched anxiously as it covered the flag through the air. After a few seconds, he heard a sharp clang.

"Congratulations, boss, we hit the cup!" exclaimed his caddie.

For years, the dent left by Crawley's shot was a source of pride to the Englishman. In fact, when it was finally removed he protested in print—with some justification.

One day Crawley was playing a match with a friend who— How shall we say this?—took certain liberties with the rules. The more it happened the angrier Crawley became, until he could no longer contain himself. As they walked off the 18th green, Crawley whacked the man on the head.

"That's for cheating all day," Crawley said. "Now let's go have a drink."

For as long as there have been golf writers there have been press junkets. Precious few writers honor the late Henry Longhurst's dictum that when dealing with tournament promoters, writers should "drink their whiskey, enjoy their women, and never write a single word about their bloody awful golf courses."

One year a group of British writers converged upon Greece for the World Cup. On a slow day, the promoters of the event arranged for a nine-island sight-seeing cruise. What they hadn't counted on was the existence of a large, inviting bar overlooking the ocean on the first island.

Coming from an island nation, the British writers figured it was the only island they needed to see. Seven hours later they stumbled out of the bar and onto the boat for the return trip.

Longhurst, who is best known in the States for his work as a CBS Sports golf commentator, was an elegant and graceful writer.

On one occasion, when writing about the difficult, par-3 18th hole at Killarney Golf Club in County Kerry, Ireland, he succinctly summed up the sheer beauty of the place.

"My, what a lovely place to die," he wrote.

One day in the late 1970s, *Golf Digest* held an advertiser outing at the Stanwich Club in the New York City suburb of Greenwich, Connecticut. It was a hot, humid day, and a combination of the weather and the generous amount of alcohol flowing from the open bars took a toll on some of the attendees—including one editor.

Following dinner Nick Seitz, who was then the magazine's editor, rose to give a short speech. As is usually the case at these sorts of outings, he praised the editorial staff, citing their unparalleled enthusiasm, energy, devotion to the game, and so on. Then he began to introduce his staff individually. His intentions were good, but his timing was not. Unknowingly, he picked just that moment to single out a senior editor who had just passed out in his chair and had unleashed a resounding snore.

It was the highlight of the outing.

One year Dick Taylor, the longtime editor of *Golf World* magazine, traveled to New Zealand to cover that country's Open championship. While he was there he was asked to serve as a television commentator, along with Australian Peter Thomson, a five-time British Open champion.

In a production meeting prior to the first day's telecast, the director told Dick that he would be responsible for profiling the foreign players.

"But I don't know any of the foreign players," he protested.

"No, Dick, you don't understand," said Thomson. "Over here, the Americans are the foreign players."

THE PRINCE OF WALES

Dealing with royalty can be a matter of some delicacy, as Willie Auchterlonie, the professional at the Royal and Ancient Golf Club of St. Andrews, discovered one day when he stepped onto the first tee to watch the Prince of Wales tee off.

A sizeable gallery had gathered around the tee, which didn't make the Prince any less nervous. He fidgeted nervously over the ball, finally took a mighty swing, and missed the ball entirely. There was an awkward silence.

"Well now, that's a fine practice swing, sir," Auchterlonie said. "Now just hit it."

The Prince of Wales actually had a hand—albeit unwittingly—in changing the rules. In 1929 he showed up for a competition at St. Andrews armed with a new set of steel-shafted clubs. At the time, the R & A still held that steel shafts were illegal. But since it would have been unseemly to disqualify the Prince of Wales, they changed the rules.

146

TED RAY

Ted Ray was the powerful Englishman who, along with compatriot Harry Vardon, dominated golf in the years before the great Americans like Bobby Jones, Walter Hagen, and Gene Sarazen came into prominence.

Ray's last win in a major came at the 1920 U.S. Open at Inverness, and he did it with style.

Standing over his putt on the final green, he suddenly walked away from the ball.

Nerves?

Hardly. His omnipresent pipe had gone out. He calmly refilled it with tobacco from an old pouch, lit it, took a few puffs, and then two-putted to win by a shot over Jack Burke, Sr., Leo Diegel, Jock Hutchison, and Harry Vardon.

BOB ROSBURG

For many years, one of the great joys of watching golf on ABC Sports was listening to the interplay between Dave Marr in the tower on 18 and Bob Rosburg down on the ground, usually with the day's final pairing. More often than not it would go something like this:

Marr: "Rossie, what's Greg got? Does he have a shot?"

Rosburg: "Dave, he's got no chance. He has a terrible lie. He's got some huge trees blocking his shot to the green and he's facing, I don't know, about 230 to the front. He's got to lay up and take his chances on making a par."

Then there'd be a pause while the player would pull off an absolutely unbelievable shot.

Rosburg: "Dave, I saw that shot but I still don't believe it. These guys are just playing a different game."

Rossie could do this because he was such a great player in his own right, the winner of the 1959 PGA Championship and five other Tour events, as well as the 1958 Vardon trophy for low scoring average.

A few years ago, Rossie was hospitalized for heart bypass surgery. The operation was successful, and after a few days of recovery, he asked his doctor how long he had to stay in the hospital. When the doctor told him, the response was pure Rossie:

"Doc, you've got no chance."

148

DOUG SANDERS

For most of his career, Doug Sanders was known for his colorful wardrobe and his willingness to party. Lost in all that was the fact that he was an enormously skilled shotmaker, especially when it came to hitting shots in the wind.

Sanders was in Scotland for the British Open one year, and following the Open stayed to play some of the classic old courses with some friends from the British Isles. One of them commented that it was a pity that, for all their skills, the American players had never mastered the bump-and-run—a staple of golf in Scotland. He picked the wrong guy.

Sanders emptied his golf bag, took out a 7-iron, and pitched a dozen or so balls to a nearby green. The ball farthest from the hole was only eighteen inches away.

SHOW BUSINESS

Golf has always attracted its share of show business celebrities. Bob Hope credits the game with his longevity, not so much because the exercise helped keep him fit, but because knowing he had a game the next morning kept him from hanging around the bar after he finished his act. Perhaps not surprisingly, very few major celebrities were actually very accomplished at the game. Hope was probably about a six-handicapper at his best. Bing Crosby was good enough to play in both the British and U.S. Amateurs, although the huge galleries he attracted embarrassed him. Sean Connery and James Garner are also very good. But for most, the game's greatest appeal is that it gives them time to relax, away from the crowds and pressures that come with celebrity.

Jack Lemmon is a passionate, if frustrated, golfer best known for his quixotic attempts to make the cut in the AT&T National Pro-Am—the old Crosby tournament—at Pebble Beach and other nearby courses.

One year back in the early 1980s, he had one of the worst possible starts to the tournament. He stood on the first tee at Pebble Beach, facing a wide-open fairway and a shortish par 4. His tee shot rocketed off to the right, through a (mercifully) open glass door and into the suite where he and his wife, Felicia, were staying. The ball caromed around the room, but didn't break anything.

Not surprisingly, given this start, he missed the cut.

Another year at the Crosby, Lemmon stood on a tee preparing to hit his drive. Just as he was about to swing, a dog burst through the gallery and ran right between Lemmon's legs. Lemmon never flinched. In fact, he hit one of his best drives of the day.

After his round he ran into a friend, who marveled that the dog hadn't upset his concentration.

"You mean that was a real dog?" Lemmon exclaimed.

Actor Victor Mature was surprised and more than a little amused when he learned that a Los Angeles newspaper had reported that he had been quietly buried in a private funeral service the previous day.

"If that's true," he told a writer for another paper, "then I'm the only guy who ever made six double bogies on the back nine on the day of his funeral."

The actress Joan Fontaine was married for a time to the Scottish golf writer Alfred Wright. During the 1965 World Cup, they found themselves on a bus returning to their hotel from a night of carousing. A number of players were singing songs from their homelands, and she approached Scotland's Eric Brown and asked if he'd be so kind as to sing a particular favorite of hers, "Home on the Range."

"Not bloody likely," he said, and promptly launched into "I Belong to Glasgow."

Ms. Fontaine joined right in.

Jim Backus, the comedian best known as the voice of the cartoon character Mr. Magoo, was a regular at the Riviera Country Club in Los Angeles. One day, when he had just finished shooting some scenes for a Roman gladiator movie for Warner Brothers, he and a friend decided to head for Riviera for a couple beers. Since they were in a hurry, they decided not to change out of their costumes.

They entered the grillroom, sat at the bar, and ordered the two drinks. The bartender cast a wary glance at them.

"What's the matter, don't you serve guys in uniform?" Backus asked.

Hillcrest Country Club, in the heart of downtown Los Angeles, has long been the favorite club of show business celebrities. That was particularly true years ago when it was the favorite club of great comedians like Jack Benny, George Burns, and Milton Berle.

For many years, the club had a rule that allowed men to play topless (the better to work on their tans) but required them to put their shirts on before they returned to the clubhouse.

This rule struck Harpo Marx as more than a little silly, so one day he followed it to what struck him as its logical conclusion. As he walked up the fairway toward the clubhouse, he dutifully put his shirt back on.

And took his pants off.

Over the years the Los Angeles Country Club has tried to avoid publicity in the most publicity-mad city in America. Its North Course is known as "the best course that's never hosted an Open," because the membership didn't want all the attention.

Perhaps it's not surprising, then, that the club has long avoided having members from the world of show business. Witness the case of Randolph Scott.

After his acting days were over, Scott became a successful businessman in Los Angeles and several of his friends sponsored him for membership at the LACC. As part of the admissions process, he was required to meet several board members, one of whom thought he looked very familiar.

"You're not an actor, are you, Mr. Scott?" the man asked.

"No," quipped Scott, "and I've got the films to prove it."

Phil Harris was playing in the Crosby Pro-Am one year. The other team in their foursome was struggling, and came to the 17th tee 18 over par. Bad enough, but the kid carrying the scoreboard had mixed up the numbers so it read 81 over par.

"Don't worry, son," Harris said. "It's still early. By the time they finish you won't have to change a thing."

Harris won the first Crosby he played in. It was 1951 and he was teamed with Dutch Harrison—a pairing of kindred spirits if there ever was one.

They came to the 17th hole on the last day, and Harris knocked in a huge putt of some eighty feet. The gallery went wild.

"You take it from here, Dutch," said Harris. "I'm heading for the bar."

He left, and Harrison made a routine par on 18 for the win.

J. C. SNEAD

For most of his career Jesse Carlyle Snead went by his initials, but for a brief stretch he let it be known that he'd prefer to be called "Jesse." That was fine, until he suddenly announced that he was going back to "J.C."

"How come?" a writer asked.

"Because Jesse isn't playing worth a damn," he answered.

Waiting to tee off one day in a pro-am, J. C. Snead was taking some practice swings, trying to get the feel for a new move he was going to try out on the course. When the starter announced his name he walked over, teed up his ball, and got into position to hit it. Then he stepped away from the ball.

"What's the matter, J.C.?" one of his pro-am partners asked.

"I forgot what I was going to try," he laughed.

SAM SNEAD

One of the oldest stories about Sam Snead stems from Jimmy Demaret's line that Sam, being a man of the mountains, didn't trust banks and buried all his money in tomato cans out in his backyard. The two got a lot of mileage from Sam's complaining that one night he awoke and found two men digging up his backyard in search of the money.

Years later, a writer asked Sam if it was true that he'd buried his money in tomato cans.

"Not tomato cans," he grinned.

Edward, Duke of Windsor, was a passionate golfer. He once asked Sam's longtime agent and friend, Fred Corcoran, if he would arrange a round of golf with Sam. Naturally, Corcoran obliged and the two men had an enjoyable round.

A few days later, the Duke telephoned Corcoran and asked if he might send a check to Sam in appreciation. Corcoran said that was very nice, but he was sure Sam would rather have an autographed photograph of the Duke. Later, when Sam found out, he quickly set the record straight.

"Next time take the check," said Sam. "If I want to start a picture collection of a bunch of kings, I can go down to Woolworth's and buy some bubble-gum cards for a nickel."

Even from his earliest days on tour, Sam was never one for hanging around a bar at night. For starters, he didn't drink, so the concept of a cover charge was alien to his way of thinking.

But in 1962, at the World Cup, he met a dozen or so players and writers at his hotel lounge following the final round. When he left for his room his friends told the waiter that "the very generous Mr. Snead had graciously agreed to pay for the drinks, so please bill his room—and while you're at it, add a generous tip for yourself."

The next morning the front desk was reduced to a standstill as the hotel management tried to explain to Sam just what this enormous bar tab was doing on his bill—and his friends looked on in amusement from the lobby.

For much of his career, Sam has been affiliated with The Greenbrier, the elegant hotel and resort in the West Virginia mountains. There, he would be available to play with the guests, usually for a little money.

There are a number of courses there, but most of his

rounds were played on the "Old White" course. The course has an odd feature: the 16th hole has two greens. The green to the right makes the hole play 394 yards. But the green to the left adds twenty yards and brings water into play.

When Sam would come to the hole, he'd announce which green they were playing to. If he was leading the match, they'd play to the right—away from the water. If he was trailing he'd give himself an edge and play to the left—figuring rightly that he had a better chance of carrying the water than his opponent did.

There never was much that got past Sam on the golf course.

People can—and will—argue about who is the greatest golfer of all time, but nobody can dispute that Sam Snead is the game's most stylish shotmaker. As Jimmy Demaret once explained to a young writer, "Son, that man hits every shot the way the rest of us would like to hit just one."

CRAIG STADLER

After winning the 1973 U.S. Amateur at Inverness, Craig Stadler was named to the 1975 Walker Cup team that would face the team from Great Britain and Ireland at St. Andrews. The Walker Cup is played under two different formats: foursomes (or alternate shot) and individual match play.

Prior to the start of the first day's foursomes play, the American captain, Dr. Ed Updegraff, announced that only two players—Curtis Strange and Jerry Pate—would play in every match. This angered a player who was scheduled to be paired with Stadler, and the player threatened to boycott the match—an unprecedented threat.

It didn't matter to Stadler, who is a particularly tough competitor under everyday circumstances and was totally fired up at the thought of representing his country in the Walker Cup matches. Stadler told his teammates that he didn't need a partner and he'd take on his opponents single-handedly.

"Everyone just kind of stood there and waited to see how Craig was going to play an alternate shot match by himself," recalls one of his teammates, Vinny Giles.

For the record, Stadler was undefeated in Walker Cup play that week, winning both his foursomes matches and his one singles match. The U.S. team went on to win, 15½ to 8½.

TITANIC THOMPSON

Alvin Clarence "Titanic" Thompson was a hustler and gambler of almost mythic proportions. He got his nickname by telling people that as a boy he escaped death in the sinking of the British luxury liner *Titanic* and that his luck never changed from that day on. But his success had less to do with luck than with an innate athleticism and an uncanny ability to figure the odds. It also helped that he had the nerves of a second-story man and a remarkable ability to judge human nature.

One of his most famous hustles came in the 1950s, and it was a work of art. You don't need to approve of what he did to appreciate the skill with which he did it.

Through the grapevine, he heard about a fine teenage player from Ohio who was nicknamed "Stick." How good was this Stick? Good enough to hold his own against another teenager named Jack Nicklaus as a junior golfer.

Anyway, Thompson called Stick, told him he had heard a lot of good things about him, and asked him to come down to Texas so Thompson could check out his game. Stick's mother was dubious about all this, to say the least, but eventually let her son head south.

When Stick got to Texas, it took just one round—a 66 on a course he'd never seen before—to convince Thompson that this kid was just who he was looking for. He told Stick to meet him in Evansville, Indiana, where Thompson had a farm adjacent to a golf course.

Stick's first job was to drive a tractor around a field next to one of the holes, and to look particularly interested in the golf when Thompson came through the hole with the club pro and some wealthy members. After several days of this, Thompson told the boy that the next time he saw Thompson's group approaching the tee, he was to get off the tractor and go sit on the fence that ran between the course and the farm—feigning a complete fascination with the golfers.

After doing this for a couple days, it was time for Thompson to take the next step in his scam.

"Say, look at that kid over there on that fence," he said to his playing companions as they played their approach shots, pointing out the rail-thin kid dressed in overalls and a straw hat and, for all we know, chewing on a piece of hay for effect. "I think he's interested in golf. He might make a good caddie."

By the end of the round, Thompson had talked the club pro into giving the kid lessons. A couple days later, Stick showed up for his first lesson. He spent the next two hours shanking, topping, whiffing, and just generally being awful. Since Stick was a naturally gifted player, these were perhaps the toughest two hours he'd ever spent on a golf course. After all, he was hitting shots he'd never hit before. Some he'd never even seen before.

The pro was willing to write the kid off as hopelessly uncoordinated and send him back to his tractor, but Thompson urged him to give it one more try. Of course, Stick began to make slow but steady progress. Soon he was even making solid contact, much to the pro's amazement.

Now it was time for the next step.

163

"You know, I'd like to give this kid a taste of competition, just to see if he likes it," Thompson told the pro and his friends. "What do you say we have a little match and I'll take the kid as my partner. He'll have to get a lot of strokes, but we won't play for much."

They agreed, and the hook was set.

The next day they went on the course, and Stick shot around 100. With his strokes, and some timely good play by Thompson, they just about broke even.

The next day they played again, and Stick improved enough so that they actually made a fair amount of money.

Now it was time for the kill. Thompson raised the stakes way up, but agreed to cut the number of strokes young Stick would get—seeing, after all, that the boy was making such amazing progress.

The next day Stick shot a 66 and they cleaned up. How much did they win? More than enough to make the hustle a very worthwhile investment in time.

Another of Titanic's better-known hustles involved tossing coins to a line on the floor. He'd bet that he could pitch three coins at a line, and that one would roll straight to the line, a second would land and kick to the right, and the third would go to the left. All three would fit under the $100 bill he held in his hand to cover his losses if he failed— which he almost never did.

PETER THOMSON

Perhaps as much as anyone who ever played, five-time British Open champion Peter Thomson made the game look simple. His swing was a model of efficency. His shot-making was crisp and precise. His ability to think his way around a course was unmatched and even the pressure of championship competition never seemed to faze him in the least. In addition, he came closer than any other player before or since to being as literate as Bobby Jones.

Given all that, it was only natural that he would be approached to write a book explaining his theories of playing the game. And so it was that he agreed to meet with Henry Longhurst on the eve of the 1959 British Open and discuss his thoughts on how to hit the ball. However, he warned Longhurst in advance, he didn't think he had enough to say to fill a book. Naturally, Longhurst attributed this to modesty.

The two met in the lounge at Rusack's Hotel in St. Andrews for two leisurely sessions. By the time the second session ended, Longhurst realized that Thomson was right. His thinking was so clear and concise that there wasn't enough cosmic mumbo-jumbo to fill a book. However, the piece he wrote detailing Thomson's thinking may still be the best golf instruction piece ever written.

LEE TREVINO

By his own admission, Lee Trevino has earned and lost several fortunes, in most cases due to mismanagement by business partners he placed too much confidence in.

This happened once, in 1976, when Trevino discovered that everything he owned—insurance policies, his home, apartments, golf courses, the works—had been used as collateral without his knowledge. Now the banks were on his case.

"That collateral is worth about as much as the paper you're holding in your hands," Trevino told the bankers. "You can't get blood from a turnip. All my contracts are based upon my playing performance, and you guys can't control my putting. If I decide to, I'll three-putt every green I look at. What are you guys going to do then?"

Lee Trevino may not have gone to Harvard Business School, but he taught some Texas bankers a lesson that day.

One day Trevino stood on a tee waiting for the pairing ahead of him to clear the green. To check the wind, he bent over and tore up a little grass, tossing it into the air.

"Excuse me, Lee," somebody from the gallery asked. "Why do you do that?"

"I don't know," Trevino joked. "I see the other guys doing it and I figure I should, too."

THE U.S. OPEN

The U.S. Open is justifiably famed—or notorious, depending on your point of view—for its narrow fairways, thick rough, and firm, fast greens. There's a temptation to think this is a modern phenomenon, but in truth, it's been this way for a very long time.

Take the case of Jock Hutchison, who won both a British Open and a PGA Championship. Coming off the course at the 1926 U.S. Open at Scioto, Ohio, he was asked about the playing conditions.

"I lost a ball in the rough today," he said. "I dropped another ball and lost that, too. Along the way I lost my caddie as well. That, gentlemen, is deep rough."

KEN VENTURI

One year Ken Venturi was playing in the San Francisco City Golf Championship, a match play tournament that drew enormous crowds and the best players in California.

In one of his matches he hit his approach putt an inch from the hole and, assuming his opponent would give him the next putt, raked the ball away.

"Ken, I didn't give you that putt," said his opponent. "Since we're playing strictly by the rules of golf, I'm afraid you lost the hole."

"If that's so, it means I'm three down with five to play," said Venturi. "Are you sure you want to win like that?"

"Well, Ken we are playing strictly by the rules," the man said.

"You're sure you want to win like that?" Venturi said.

"The rules are the rules, Ken."

"Okay, you've got fifteen clubs in your bag," said Venturi, heading for the clubhouse. "I win."

TOM WEISKOPF

Tom Weiskopf is one of the most stylish golfers ever to play on tour. Not only was his shotmaking impressive, but he took great pride in his clothes—in no small part due to the influence of Tommy Bolt early in his career. It was Bolt, after all, who insisted that you were allowed to walk off the course in mid-round if your pants lost their crease.

One afternoon Weiskopf was being interviewed over lunch by a *Golf Digest* writer, Guy Yocom, for a story about the 1975 Masters, where Weiskopf, Jack Nicklaus, and Johnny Miller staged a classic duel on the final day. Nicklaus won after sinking a thirty-five-foot birdie putt on 16 and then watched from the scorer's tent as both Miller and Weiskopf barely missed birdie putts on the last hole. Many people consider it one of the greatest Masters ever played, if not *the* greatest.

In all, Weiskopf finished second four times, but by his own admission 1975 was the toughest loss of them all—"the one that killed me," he admits.

In the course of the interview, Weiskopf talked about the sweater he had worn in the last round of the 1975 Masters.

"I had all my sweaters custom made in Scotland," he said. "This one was kind of my lucky sweater, if you know what I mean. I had worn it in the finals of the 1972 World Match

Play in England when I killed Lee Trevino. After that Masters, I put it in my closet and never wore it again in competition. I still, you know, take it out and look at it and I might wear it socially, but never—never—again in competition."

"That's amazing, Tom," said Yocom. "Was it a cashmere sweater?"

Weiskopf almost choked on his lunch.

"Jesus Christ, Guy, of course it was cashmere," he sputtered. "You don't think I'd have a polyester sweater custom made, do you? I mean, Jesus, Guy, how could you even think I'd wear polyester?"

Weiskopf's sense of style even extended to what other players wore. One year at the Masters, he was standing near the clubhouse, overlooking the first tee, with fellow announcer Gary McCord and some other friends.

"Tom, take a look at this guy," said McCord. "Tell me what you think of his swing."

Weiskopf looked over at the tee and then looked away disdainfully.

"I'm not looking at his swing," said Weiskopf.

"Why not?" asked McCord.

"I'm not looking at anyone's swing who wears Dockers at the Masters," he explained.

One day Tom Weiskopf was having sequence photographs taken of his swing for *Golf Digest*. The course was busy, which meant that groups were constantly asking to play through the hole where the photos were being taken. After yet another delay of several minutes, Weiskopf turned to the editor and photographer assigned to the shoot.

"Is this the last ball I have to hit?" he asked. "I'm starting to lose interest."

"This better be the last ball," said one of Weiskopf's friends, who was standing nearby. "I've seen him lose interest. It's not pretty."

In 1964 Tom Weiskopf, then a twenty-one-year old amateur, traveled with a friend to Washington to watch the U.S. Open at Congressional Country Club. In the first group they watched, one player hit a big hook off the tee. The next player hit an equally ugly slice.

"Jesus, I can play better than these guys," he said to his friend. "I'm turning pro."

He did, and thirty-one years later returned to Congressional to win the U.S. Senior Open.

It is one of the oddities of Tom Weiskopf's career that some of his greatest triumphs have come at times of personal sadness. His two best years on the PGA Tour came following the deaths of his father and his golf coach at Ohio State, Bob Kepler. He won the Senior Open—his only real goal on the Senior Tour—while his wife fought breast cancer, and his first official win on the Senior Tour came just days after the death of his best friend on tour throughout his career, Bert Yancey.

Yancey and Weiskopf were in Utah for the 1994 Franklin Quest Championship. Just prior to teeing off in the first round, Yancey suffered a heart attack and died. Weiskopf was shattered, and was ready to pull out of the tournament, but instead decided to dedicate the tournament to Yancey.

Trailing Dave Stockton in the final round, Weiskopf birdied three of the last five holes to force a playoff. Then, at the awards ceremony, he asked that Yancey's name be engraved on the trophy next to his own.

"I honestly felt that Bert was with me that day," Weiskopf said later. "I could actually hear him repeating some of the things he always told me—you know, little tips. I wanted his name on the trophy so he'd never be forgotten."

Yancey suffered from manic depression, an illness made worse by his doctors' inability to prescribe the proper medication for much of his career.

One year, at the Westchester Classic, he and Weiskopf were paired together. It didn't take long for Weiskopf to sense that something was wrong with his old friend.

"He arrived on the tee needing a shave and his clothes were a mess," Weiskopf remembers. "This was before he'd been diagnosed as a manic depressive, so none of us really knew what was wrong with him. As the round went on, he began to act stranger and stranger. Finally, I couldn't take it anymore. I walked off the course and went to find a rules official. The next day it was in all the papers that I had quit and just walked off the course. CBS, which was doing the telecast, crucified me. Nobody knew the real reason.

"One good thing that came out of it was that I vowed never to walk off the course again," he went on. "A little kid came up to me as I came out of the clubhouse. He had tears streaming down his face. He said that his father had taken him out of school just to see me, and that I was his hero. I was shattered. I mean, how do you explain something like this to a kid? I promised him I'd never walk off the course again—and I never did."

Tom Weiskopf is a gifted golf course designer, and one of his greatest works is Loch Loman, which many people believe is the best inland course in Scotland. Ironically, Weiskopf's dedication to detail and his love of the course almost cost him his life in 1991.

He and his wife, Jeannie, were staying in a cottage at Loch Loman. One night, sleeping fitfully, Weiskopf decided to go out and look over the 14th hole, which he didn't feel was set up quite right. Not wanting to wake Jeannie, he dressed quietly and headed for the course.

The course was empty, and would be for several hours until the work crews arrived. In the darkness, Weiskopf made his way out to the hole. But before he got there, he slid into a bog and quickly sank to his waist. He could feel his boots being pulled from his feet as he struggled to avoid being sucked deeper into the bog. But the harder he fought to escape, the deeper he sank. Soon he was up to his armpits, and had come to the grim realization that he might well die in the bog and never be found.

His cries for help echoing over the empty course, he struggled to find a way to keep from sinking further. Beyond panic now, he found that if he moved in a certain way he could make progress toward solid ground. He reached for some long grass, but the sharp blades slashed his hands and soon they were bleeding badly. Still, he was making headway. If he could just hang on until the workers arrived, he'd be saved. But that was still hours away.

Determined to survive, Weiskopf exhausted all his strength struggling to pull himself free. Finally, after some four hours, he escaped and collapsed beside the bog, utterly exhausted.

After resting and regaining some strength, he staggered back to the cottage. His boots and jeans had been pulled from his body. His hands were bloody messes. He was caked with muddy slime.

When Jeannie asked what had happened, he said simply that he'd slipped and fallen. Then he showered and went to bed, and slept for a solid ten hours.

JACK WHITAKER

It's ironic that Jack Whitaker is best known in golf, not for his lyrical essays and commentary that reflect his love and understanding of the game, but for an incident that brings credit to neither Augusta National nor CBS Sports.

In 1966, during Clifford Roberts's autocratic reign as chairman of Augusta National, Whitaker described the galleries charging up the 18th fairway at the close of the Monday playoff between Jack Nicklaus, Tommy Jacobs, and Gay Brewer, as a "mob." Roberts, exerting the leverage that is a part and parcel of Augusta's one-year contracts with CBS, demanded and received Whitaker's expulsion from the Masters telecasts for the next six years.

In the course of his career, Whitaker has received two Emmy awards for broadcasting excellence. In 1995, he was honored for his contributions to journalism at a dinner in the New York suburbs. In an emotional thank-you, he summed up his career with the grace that has always been his trademark:

"A lot of times you look at your life and wonder if you should have done something else," he said. "You wonder if you should have done something to contribute more to society, maybe teaching or politics. But now, looking back, I realize that I leaned my ladder against the right wall. Now I know that I did what was right, and I am eternally grateful for the chance to have done it with such marvelous people."

"ACE" WILLIAMS

A rthur "Ace" Williams is a fine senior golfer from Connecticut. In his younger days he played in a lot of the
bigger amateur events in the New York area. One that he
particularly enjoyed was the Anderson Memorial, a team
event at Winged Foot Golf Club.

"I was playing with a friend one year and we tied with
another team in the qualifying rounds for match play,"
Williams remembers. "We had to play off for the last spot,
but it was too dark, so we had to come back the next morning. The playoff began on the 10th hole on the West Course,
a very difficult par 3. One of our opponents hit it in very
close for a certain birdie. My partner hit a poor shot, but I
got lucky and made a hole-in-one.

"Several years later I was at a club in Florida and I heard
a man telling a story about the time he 'was playing in the
Anderson and some lucky son of a bitch made a hole-in-one
on the 10th to beat him in a playoff.'"

"I went over, shook his hand, and said, 'I'm the lucky son
of a bitch who beat you in the playoff.'"

179

MORRIS WILLIAMS

Most golf fans know that Tom Kite and Ben Crenshaw grew up competing against each other as teenagers in Austin, Texas, and later as students at the University of Texas. But as good as they are, many people believe that Morris Williams was as good, if not better.

Like Kite and Crenshaw, Williams was a pupil of the late Harvey Penick. At age thirteen, Williams became the youngest person ever to win the Austin City Championship and went on to dominate area golf.

Like Kite and Crenshaw, Williams went to the University of Texas, leading his team to the Southwest Conference titles in 1947, '49, and '50. In his senior year he finished second in the NCAA individual competition.

After graduating, Williams joined the Air Force and won every interservice tournament he played in, including the worldwide Air Force championship in 1959. Not long after winning that tournament he was killed in a crash during a training flight.

"I was at Austin Country Club when I got the call telling me that Morris had been killed," remembered Harvey Penick. "I had to be the one to break the news to his father, and it was the hardest thing I've ever had to do in my life. He was the sports editor of the Austin paper. When he came into the newsroom he asked me what I was doing there. I started to tell him but broke into tears. I barely managed to get the words out and Mr. Williams collapsed in my arms."

WIVES AND LOVERS

There are some reasons for getting a divorce that are better than others. Take the example of the man who had given his wife his entry for the U.S. Open. Things hadn't been going very well in their marriage for some time, and in the midst of yet another heated argument, she told him that instead of mailing his entry to the USGA, she had thrown it away.

That was more than the man could stand. He picked up the phone, called his lawyer, and started divorce proceedings.

"My wife always said she wanted to marry a millionaire," joked Chi Chi Rodriguez one day. "Well, I have to give her credit. She made me a millionaire. Of course, I used to be a multimillionaire."

"We took a mulligan."
　　　　—PGA Tour pro Bill Kratzert, on his marriage,
　　　　divorce, and remarriage to his wife, Cheryl

When Nick Faldo was divorced from his first wife, a friend asked if he'd always been unhappy in the marriage.

"No, I was very happily married for two years," he said. "Unfortunately, we were married for seven."

There is a man in Connecticut who collected golf clubs for most of his adult life. He had clubs in closets. He had them in his basement. In his garage. In his attic. Every place you could keep clubs, he had them stashed there—much to his wife's dismay.

Finally, after years of listening to his long-suffering wife, he agreed to sell his entire collection. The $50,000 he received helped make him feel a little better about the whole business. . .

. . . until he found out that the dealer he sold them to turned around and sold the collection for a cool $1 million.

Corey Pavin met his wife, Shannon, when he was a student at UCLA. One day he noticed her gazing at him from across a crowded room. Naturally, he was flattered and took this as a sign that she was interested in meeting him.

It wasn't until later that he discovered she wasn't wearing her contacts and couldn't see him at all.

When Ralph Guldahl won the 1937 U.S. Open at Oakland Hills, his first-place check was $2,000. His wife, LaVerne, always loved horses, and she talked her husband into buying one with his winnings. The second time she rode the horse, she fell off and broke her arm. That was it for Mrs. Guldahl's horse. She gave it away.

Reporters asked former First Lady Barbara Bush for her reaction to the news that her husband was going to play in the Bob Hope Desert Classic along with President Clinton and former President Gerald Ford.

"Isn't there already enough violence and bloodshed on television?" she said.

Men-only golf clubs are becoming increasingly rare in the United States, but one that remains staunchly so is Bob O'Link, outside Chicago. A member once described the club this way: "It's like a family club without women."

TIGER WOODS

Tiger Woods, who won the U.S. Amateur in both 1994 and 1995 while still a teenager, was paired with Curtis Strange in the second round of the 1995 Masters. On the 5th hole Woods crushed a drive that measured 347 yards.

"Tiger, I'm just gonna retire and watch you play golf," said Curtis.

"You've been a hero of mine since I was a kid," Woods said, respectfully, to the two-time U.S. Open champion.

"You ain't a kid anymore," said Curtis.

BEN WRIGHT

British-born golf commentator Ben Wright is part of an increasingly rare breed—a television journalist who got his start in newspapering. His entry into television came in the early 1970s when fellow Englishman Henry Longhurst was taken ill and CBS's golf producer, Frank Chirkinian, went looking for a replacement Brit. He found Ben, who's been a regular member of the CBS broadcast team until recently.

As a young man, Ben Wright enjoyed driving race cars—until he was involved in a serious accident. The accident caused serious damage to his mouth, and he was required to wear false teeth.

One morning, in Los Angeles for the telecast of the L.A. Open, he was seized with a coughing fit. Somehow, his upper plate fell into the toilet just as it was being flushed. To his utter shock, he watched his teeth—and possibly his career—head for the Los Angeles sewer system. There were just scant hours before he was scheduled to go on the air.

In a panic, he called the production truck and explained his dilemma. CBS found a dentist nearby, who came up with a temporary replacement plate to get Wright through the telecast.

Of course, if he thought he was going to get off that eas-

187

ily, he was sadly mistaken. As he began to record his taped hole opener ("I'm Ben Wright, and I shall be reporting play from the . . ."), his producer told him to look at the monitor, where a set of windup false teeth went chattering across the screen.

FUZZY ZOELLER

On the eve of his playoff with Greg Norman in the 1984 U.S. Open at Winged Foot, Fuzzy Zoeller and his wife went out to dinner. As it turned out, Norman and his wife were at the same restaurant. Fuzzy had an expensive bottle of wine sent to the Normans' table.

As the Zoellers were leaving, they stopped at the Normans' table.

"Did you like that wine?" Fuzzy asked.

"Very much," said Norman. "It was excellent."

"Well, have as many bottles as you'd like," Fuzzy joked. "On me."

It's not clear if the Normans took Fuzzy up on his offer, but the results of the next day's playoff suggest that they might have. Zoeller shot a 67. Norman skied to a 74.

INDEX

192

195